THE STRUGGLE FOR FREEDOM

Plays on the American Revolution, 1762–1788

by Charles F. Baker III

ABOUT THE COVER

"I have not yet begun to fight", declared John Paul Jones, commander of the American ship *Bon Homme Richard*, when asked to surrender during the savage battle against the British ships *Serapis* and *Countess of Scarborough*, on September 23, 1779. His ship in flames, Jones fought on and finally defeated the British. The cover painting is by Richard Paton and is reproduced courtesy of the United States Naval Academy Museum.

Copy-edited by Lou Waryncia

Designed by C. Porter Designs

Illustrations by Joyce Audy Zarins

Maps by Coni Porter

Typesetting by Sally Nichols Jacke

Printing and Binding by The William Byrd Press, Inc.

Manufactured in the United States of America

ISBN 0-942389-05-0

Cobblestone Publishing, Inc.
30 Grove Street
Peterborough, NH 03458

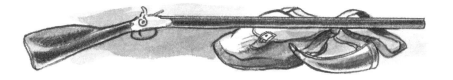

CONTENTS

(Continued on next page)

For my wife, Rosalie, and my son, Chip

Foreword

The Revolutionary War period was a unique time in U.S. history. The struggle for freedom bonded together people from all professions and social classes. Men, women, and children willingly performed heroic deeds with little thought about themselves. Freedom from England, the oppressor, was the common tie that joined them.

The period from 1762 to **1788** is well documented. The details of that time, however, were usually written long after the incidents or events occurred. Some incidents were recorded by friends, relatives, or acquaintances of eyewitnesses or participants. Often multiple accounts were recorded, with each person writing down his or her own viewpoint. As a result, the historical records differ—sometimes slightly, other times almost to the point of contradiction.

In researching the material for the plays in this book, the author used facts generally agreed upon by historians. When historians disagreed, the most widely accepted version was chosen. The times and the circumstances were kept in mind as much as possible when creating the dialogue, as was the audience for whom the plays were written.

History, especially that of one's own country, can be exciting and rewarding, instilling a sense of pride and belonging. Reading historical plays helps make events of the past real, transporting the reader to the time of the action and creating a closeness between the reader and the characters. The purpose of this book is to nurture in young Americans an appreciation of the men, women, and children who, centuries ago, sacrificed so much to create a free United States for all of us.

Charles F. Baker III

The Eastern United States in 1763

Colonists vs. Native A

COLONISTS VS. NATIVE AMERICANS

Historical Overview

In May 1607, after five storm-tossed months at sea, three small English ships, the *Godspeed*, the *Susan Constant*, and the *Discovery*, reached Virginia in the New World. The passengers were settlers who had been sent by a group of London merchants. These businessmen were determined to establish a permanent colony in the New World in order to begin a successful trading venture.

The new colonists settled in the Chesapeake Bay area and named their settlement Jamestown after their king, James I. Life was harsh for the colonists, especially since so many of the newcomers were not used to working the fields, building houses, or chopping wood. Disease and other hardships took many lives, but the colony survived and grew. A body of representatives was established to pass laws that would govern land control and colonists' rights. Unfortunately, the rights of the Indians whose lands the colonists had invaded were often disregarded.

In 1620, another group of English subjects, known as Pilgrims, obtained permission from the government to settle in Virginia. During the voyage, their ship, the *Mayflower*, went off course and landed on the shores of what is now Plymouth, Massachusetts. In 1630, a third group of English people, whose beliefs gave them the name Puritans, sailed across the Atlantic and landed on the shores of Massachusetts Bay.

Despite difficult winters and a shortage of food and necessities, these colonies grew and prospered. Eventually, more and more settlers crossed the Atlantic to America. By 1757, one hundred fifty years after the founding of the Jamestown colony, almost two million people lived in Colonial America. Most of these settlers were English, but a great number had emigrated from other European countries and many were slaves who had been brought from Africa.

People emigrated to the New World for different reasons. The freedom to practice religion, business and professional opportunities, and land ownership were some of the dominant reasons.

As more colonists arrived, land seekers kept traveling farther inland to stake their claims. These lands were populated by various Indian tribes that had claimed them hundreds of years earlier. As a result, the colonists and the Indians, who both believed they owned the lands, often resorted to bloodshed to resolve their conflicts. Some colonists befriended the Indians, and they lived together peacefully. The relationship between the Indians and the newcomers varied from area to area and decade to decade.

But the English were not the only newcomers to America. English territorial claims reached only from the Atlantic Ocean on the east to the Appalachian Mountains on the west. The lands to the south (present-day Florida) were claimed by Spain, and those to the west across the Appalachians and bordering the Mississippi River were claimed by France. Since France and England were long-time enemies and had fought each other in many wars, their claims in the New World set the stage for another major confrontation, the French and Indian War.

In 1752, the French began to build forts along the border of western Pennsylvania, an area also claimed by England. In 1754, the governor of Virginia ordered George Washington to lead a band of soldiers into the Ohio River valley and build a fort there. The French had already built Fort Duquesne in that area, and they succeeded in chasing Washington and his troops out of the territory.

The Indians watched the struggle between the British and the French with great interest. When the French defeated Washington's troops, most Indians chose to ally themselves with the French. The Indians also felt more secure with the French because they were fur traders and not land investors or settlers like the British.

For several years, the Indians' choice proved advantageous. Then, in 1757, William Pitt became the new prime minister of Britain. He ordered more troops and supplies sent to the British colonists. Gradually the tide of the struggle began to turn. France eventually surrendered, and the Treaty of Paris was signed in 1763 ending the French and Indian War. According to the terms of the treaty, France ceded to Britain all of Canada and all territory east of the Mississippi River. The city of New Orleans, the port of New Orleans, and the Louisiana Territory were ceded to Spain.

To prevent further bloodshed and to promote better relations between the English, the colonists, and the Indians, the Proclamation Line of 1763 was passed. This law reserved the land west of the Appalachian Mountains for the Indians, forbade colonists to cross the Proclamation Line, and ordered those who had crossed it to retreat east of the line.

Many settlers felt that the Proclamation Line was a violation of their rights as colonists, not a means of keeping peace with the Indians. Many disregarded the Proclamation Line and pushed westward. Land company representatives and land developers were the worst offenders. The Indians, who had allied themselves with the French, watched as their land was invaded by a steady flow of settlers who rarely respected the Indians' rights and often engaged in dishonest trade.

To survive as Indian nations and to keep possession of their lands, it was necessary for the Indians to unite and push back the invaders. An Indian named Pontiac proposed to do just that. His task was especially difficult, for success depended on his ability to unite all the Indian tribes and to keep them together until they won. The following play is based on Pontiac's struggles to keep Indian lands for the Indians.

Chief Pontiac's Conspiracy

Characters

Pontiac — a great Ottawa chief who has united many tribes against the British

Macapacelite — Pontiac's war chief

Delaware Prophet —an old Indian man who preaches that the Indians should return to the ways of their forefathers

Major Gladwin — the British commander of Fort Detroit

French Interpreter — the Frenchman who acts as the interpreter at Fort Detroit for the Indians and the British

Soldier — a British soldier from Fort Sandusky

Officer — a British officer at Fort Detroit

Chief of the Potawatomi
Chief of the Chippewa
Chief of the Huron

Introduction

Narrator 1: According to legend, Pontiac, the great leader of the Indian tribes of the East, was born of an Ottawa mother and a Chippewa father around 1720 in an Ottawa village located on the Detroit River between Lake Erie and Lake Huron. He grew into an intelligent, strong-willed adult with a commanding physical appearance that impressed everyone who met him.

When Pontiac became a chief, the lands he loved—the primeval forests where he had played as a child and hunted as a young man—were changing rapidly. More and more white men and women were settling in the interior of the continent. The scattered camps of French trappers, whom the Indians tolerated for many years, had gradually been replaced by forts and settlements.

After the British conquered Montreal in 1760, they continued to take over French forts on the western Great Lakes, bringing more settlers with them. By 1762, Pontiac was firmly convinced that the British were treating the Indians worse than the French had treated them. His greatest concern was that the British provided the Indians with only a small amount of gunpowder. Since the Indians had come to rely on guns to hunt for food, this was a very serious problem. The British, quite naturally, did not want the Indians to use the gunpowder to kill white people. The Indians resented this distrustful attitude.

A few Indian tribes had tried to organize a war against the British, but the attempt was not successful because other tribes had not supported them. In order to have the strength to regain their lands and their independence, all the Indians needed to unite.

The time had come for a strong leader to gather the tribes together. This was the opportunity for which Pontiac had been waiting.

Act I, Scene 1

Narrator 1: It is late in the year 1762. British settlers are arriving in increasing numbers in the Ohio River valley, and their settlements are spreading deep into the lands that for generations belonged to the Delaware Indians. An old Indian known as the Delaware Prophet mysteriously appears in the valley and advises the Indians to abandon the customs of the white man and return to the ways of their ancestors. The Prophet's message has come at the right moment. Chief Pontiac is ready to gather all his people together in an effort to strike at the British.

Pontiac travels to a Delaware village in the Ohio Valley to visit the elderly Delaware Prophet. The tall, muscular chief, an imposing figure with colored beads in his pierced ears and nose and several silver bracelets on his powerful arms, appears at the entrance to the old man's hut. The Prophet, dressed simply in contrast with Pontiac, is sitting quietly on a rug of furs.

Delaware Prophet: Come into my humble dwelling, mighty chief. I have been expecting you.

Narrator 2: Pontiac, because of his great height, has to bend down to enter.

Pontiac: *(standing before the mystic)* How did you know to expect me? I have just arrived in your village.

Prophet: I am not known as a prophet for nothing. I often have visions, and I knew you were coming.

Pontiac: Do you know the reason for my visit?

Prophet: I will leave that up to you to tell me.

Pontiac: I have heard that you talk to the Great Spirit. The message you have been preaching throughout the valley appeals to me. My thoughts have been similar. I would like to know more.

Prophet: Sit down beside me. I will tell you willingly, for my story is meant for you to hear. The Great Spirit needs courageous men to carry out his wishes.

Narrator 2: Pontiac sits on the furs in front of the old man and waits for him to begin. The Prophet closes his eyes and appears to go into a trance. After several minutes, he begins to speak slowly.

Prophet: About a year ago, I had the desire to speak to the Great Spirit. I had been taught how to do this by my father, who also was known as a prophet. I began fasting, and the dreams came as I was told they would. I then chanted the magical songs I was taught as a child. Soon I traveled in my mind to the lodge of the Great Spirit. He bid me enter and gave me his message, for it was he who had summoned me and not I who had wanted to speak to him.

Pontiac: What did he say?

Prophet: He told me that he was the creator of heaven and earth and of all things living and dead. He said that he loved me and that because of this, I must do what he asked.

Narrator 2: The old man pauses. He is perspiring, even though the small hut is bitterly cold.

Pontiac: What did the Great Spirit ask of you?

> *"Go now and fulfill your dream, for you have been chosen by the Great Spirit to carry out his wishes."*

Prophet: He told me that he had created the lands on which we live and that they were meant only for the Indians, not for white men to inhabit. He told me that our people have forgotten the ways and traditions of our ancestors. He asked me why we now use guns instead of the bow and arrow to hunt for food and why we have bought knives, iron pots, and blankets from the white man instead of using quartz rocks, gourds, and furs. He told me to tell my people to abandon the customs and things of the white man. He commanded me to drive them from our lands.

Pontiac: This is a message dear to my heart, for it has been my dream these past several years to win back the land of my ancestors. You have already spread this word among many tribes. I will now have the blessing of the Great Spirit behind my efforts to unite our brothers and sisters into one people. Our purpose will be to drive out the British who have occupied our lands and have taken our identity from us.

Prophet: Go now and fulfill your dream, for you have been chosen by the Great Spirit to carry out his wishes. I am but his messenger. Do not fail him.

Pontiac: I will do my best.

Prophet: But spare the French. They have been our friends.

Pontiac: This I know. They will be our allies against the British. We will need all the support we can get.

Prophet: May the Great Spirit be with you.

Narrator 2: Pontiac rises and leaves. The old man immediately falls asleep, spent from his exhausting ordeal. The chief returns to his village so he can call together a council of tribes.

Act I, Scene 2

Narrator 1: The Ottawa village of Pontiac several days later. The chief is determined to take the advice of the Prophet and put into motion a plan to free the Indians. Pontiac sends for his war chief, Macapacelite, who enters Pontiac's hut.

Pontiac: Greetings, my brother. I have just returned from a meeting with the famous Delaware Prophet, and I am anxious to share my news with you.

Macapacelite: I was surprised that you came back so soon.

Pontiac: I did not want to waste any time. Sit down and let me tell you my story.

Narrator 2: Pontiac joins the war chief next to the fire and relates his tale. Macapacelite listens carefully and becomes noticeably excited.

Macapacelite: Then the rumors we have heard about the Prophet are true. This is the Great Spirit's blessing that we need to begin our war against the British.

Pontiac: The Prophet has already aroused many Indians. I want you to send messengers to all the tribes in the Ohio Valley to come for a council meeting on the banks of the Ecorse River this spring after the weather is better for traveling and all the crops have been planted. That will give us time to form our plans.

Macapacelite: Whom should I notify?

Pontiac: The chiefs of the Chippewa, Huron, and Potawatomi and all the other chiefs of the tribes in our area. We need all the support we can get.

Macapacelite: I will send the messenger at once.

Pontiac: We will begin our battle plans when you return.

Pontiac feels powerful when he stands looking out over the hundreds of Indians before him.

Narrator 2: Soon Pontiac and his war chief, inspired and encouraged by the mysterious Prophet, begin to organize a conspiracy against the British.

Act II, Scene 1

Narrator 1: It is early spring. Throughout the winter, Pontiac has received the assurance he needs from the other chiefs and tribes that they are willing to unite under his command. The Indians are all aware that now is the time to act. They begin preparing to journey to the appointed secret meeting place.

Pontiac and Macapacelite have formulated a plan to attack the British. They are anxious to assemble all the tribes together. They meet in Pontiac's hut to discuss the gathering.

Pontiac: Macapacelite, have we heard from all the tribes?

Macapacelite: Yes, Pontiac, and they are all prepared to meet with you at the end of this month.

Pontiac: Have we heard yet whether or not the French will be our allies? They should, for the Delaware Prophet and I have been spreading the word that the French are our friends.

Macapacelite: I received word from some French traders that their country's troops in Louisiana will support us.

Pontiac: That is great news! The other tribes will have more confidence in our plan of action if we have this additional military assistance. What have you heard from the tribes to the west?

Macapacelite: War belts decorated with the message that the great Seneca tribe is ready to join us against the British have been circulating among the tribes.

Pontiac: We can only succeed now. I am ready to act! We have the support to attack all the British forts in our area in a sudden, unified uprising. We must take the white people by surprise and with strength in numbers. Prepare our warriors for the journey to the spot where all the tribes have agreed to meet.

Narrator 2: Macapacelite leaves to carry out Pontiac's wishes, and the village soon comes alive with the excitement of the anticipated battles.

Act II, Scene 2

Narrator 1: More than four hundred chiefs and warriors from tribes that live in the area between Lake Ontario and the Mississippi River are gathered in a broad treeless valley on the banks of the Ecorse River. They are determined to win back the lands of their ancestors.

There are also several Frenchmen present, all of whom Pontiac specifically invited. They are amazed and frightened by the large number of Indians who have assembled for the most important council ever to be held on the continent.

The meeting has been kept a secret. The British, who are located at Fort Detroit only six miles away, do not even suspect that the council is being held. Indian guards have been stationed around the valley so that no Englishmen can accidentally come upon the assembly.

The air, quivering with the sounds of bells, drums, rattles, and the excited talk of the Indians, becomes still when Pontiac climbs the hill overlooking the valley to address his brothers. Pontiac feels powerful when he stands looking out over the hundreds of Indians before him. He feels the spirit of his forefathers.

Pontiac: My brothers and our French friends, it is the wish of the Great Spirit that we are gathered here today. We have suffered long enough since the British have inhabited our lands. Through the years, we have lost our identity and our self-respect. I have heard from the Delaware Prophet that the Great Spirit is unhappy with us. We have allowed the land that he gave to our ancestors to be taken from us, and we have forgotten the ways of our forefathers. The British do not belong here. They have their own country. It is up to us to force them to return to the lands the Great Spirit made for them. I say that we should declare war on the British.

Narrator 2: The hundreds of Indians before him let out a war whoop.

Chief of the Chippewa: *(after the warriors have quieted down)* Does the Great Spirit feel the same way about the French?

Pontiac: He has no ill feelings toward the French. They are our brothers because they have treated us fairly and have trusted us.

Chief of the Chippewa: The Chippewa are ready to follow you, Pontiac. What are your plans?

Pontiac: We must first attack Fort Detroit.

Chief of the Huron: But it is such a sturdy and well-defended fort.

Pontiac: All the more reason to take it first. Such a victory will be a great blow to the British.

Chief of the Potawatomi: The British are well supplied and can probably hold out against us for weeks until reinforcements come to their aid.

Pontiac: We must surprise them. In four days, I plan to take fifty of my warriors and ask permission to enter the fort by offering to entertain the soldiers. While we are performing a ceremonial dance, some of us will sneak away and spy on the British to discover their weaknesses. Then we will return and form a plan of attack that will take place at a later date with other nearby tribes.

Chief of the Chippewa: What are the rest of us to do in the meantime?

Pontiac: Those of you who live far away must return to your villages and prepare your weapons for war. When you have heard that we have destroyed Fort Detroit, you will turn on the British in your own lands and drive them out. Do not be afraid because the French will send troops from Louisiana to help us.

Chief of the Huron: I have had my doubts about your plan, but we will do as you command, Pontiac. No other chief has gathered so many tribes and Indians together against the British and won the support of the French. If we are ever going to reclaim our lands and gain back our respect, it is now.

Pontiac: We are united in a common cause, and we have the blessing of the Great Spirit. It is up to us not to disappoint him. Now return to your villages and get ready for war. Do not let the English learn of our plans. If we are to succeed, we must take them by surprise.

Narrator 2: The Indians let out a roar of approval and then return to their campsites. The chiefs individually approach Pontiac and give him their support.

Act III, Scene 1

Narrator 1: It is later in the spring. The Indians are anxious to attack Fort Detroit, the largest and strongest fort in the West. Pontiac, Macapacelite, and about fifty warriors approach the main gate of Fort Detroit acting very relaxed, laughing, and dancing about as if they were going to a celebration. They are not carrying weapons. Instead, many of the Indians have pouches of tobacco and clay peace pipes with them. Several British soldiers and a French interpreter meet the Indians outside the gate. Pontiac and Macapacelite step forward to speak to the French interpreter, who, with several soldiers, is standing in the gateway blocking the entrance to the fort. He asks permission to enter the fort with his warriors. Major Gladwin, the commander of Fort Detroit, is suspicious of the Indians because he was informed of the big council they had on the Ecorse River the week before.

Pontiac: We come in peace. It is our custom each spring to dance for the commander of this fort and smoke the peace pipe with him as a declaration of our friendship with the English. May we enter?

French Interpreter: Major Gladwin, our new commander, is not familiar with all the local customs. I must first ask his permission.

Pontiac: (*determined to get into the fort*) We will wait here for his answer.

Narrator 2: The interpreter goes back inside the fort to speak to the commander. Minutes later, he returns to the gate.

Pontiac: Will the major honor our request?

Interpreter: Yes, you may all enter and perform your ceremony for Major Gladwin and his soldiers on the parade ground in front of his house.

Pontiac: *(turning to his warriors with a gleam in his eye)* Now, my restless braves, we will show the new commander how well we dance.

Narrator 2: Pontiac and his warriors follow the interpreter into the fort.

Act III, Scene 2

Narrator 1: The parade ground in front of Major Gladwin's house. The commander and his officers are waiting on the porch for the great chief. The warriors arrange themselves in a circle and prepare for the ceremonial dance. As a crowd of soldiers, women, and children gather around the Indians, Macapacelite and a few warriors slip away to spy on the British and discover the strengths and weaknesses of the fortress while their brothers are dancing. The major then steps forward to greet Pontiac with the French interpreter by his side to translate for both men.

Major Gladwin: Welcome to Fort Detroit, Chief Pontiac. I have wanted to meet you. Your reputation as a wise and courageous chief has preceded your visit.

Pontiac: My chiefs, warriors, and I wish to demonstrate our friendship to you and all the English by performing a ceremonial dance and then by sharing the peace pipe with you.

Gladwin: I accept your most gracious offer. We are honored by your visit and value your friendship. We desire peace with all Indians. My people are also in much need of entertainment, as you can see by the curious crowd that has gathered

> *We are united in a common cause, and we have the blessing of the Great Spirit.*

around you. Please proceed with your ceremony.

Pontiac: *(turning to his warriors)* Begin the dancing!

Narrator 2: The Indians, led by Pontiac, dance in a circle with much leaping and whirling about for as long as they can in order to give Macapacelite and his men time to gather crucial information for their future attack. After more than an hour has passed, the Indians collapse and the missing men slip into the circle, their absence unnoticed. Pontiac then walks forward with a red clay pipe to share with the major as the other warriors take out their peace pipes and light them.

Pontiac: *(holding out the pipe to Major Gladwin)* I give you this pipe as a symbol of friendship between our people.

Gladwin: *(taking the pipe and smiling cautiously)* I gladly accept any offer of peace. We will give you some bread and tobacco in return for your efforts and as a token of the friendship between your people and mine.

Pontiac: I would like to bring more of my people to meet you in a week's time.

Narrator 2: Pontiac's request arouses Major Gladwin's suspicions, but he does not want to dampen the friendly atmosphere created by the day's celebration.

Gladwin: That can be arranged.

Pontiac: *(visibly pleased)* Then we will return next week for a larger, more formal gathering of our people.

Narrator 2: Pontiac turns and leads his warriors out of the fort, anxious to learn what information Macapacelite and his men have discovered. They return to the council area on the Ecorse River to discuss the next stage of their war plans. It is hoped that they have had time to discover the enemy's weaknesses.

Act III, Scene 3

Narrator 1: Pontiac's campsite in the valley on the Ecorse River where the council has been meeting. It is evening, and the chief is discussing the next step of the plan to destroy Fort Detroit with Macapacelite and the other chiefs.

Pontiac: Macapacelite, what strengths and weaknesses did you and your men observe in the fort?

Macapacelite: The fort is large and well made. The village within is surrounded by a fence of pointed cedar logs fifteen feet high. There are three structures at three of its corners that project from the wall so that defenders can fire at attackers from several angles. There are also two small blockhouses not connected to the barricade. All the walls and buildings are in very good condition. It is obvious that recent repairs have been made.

Pontiac: We must not underestimate this new commander, Major Gladwin. I have heard that he has experience fighting the French and their Indian friends. He must suspect trouble if he has kept the fort in such good repair.

Chief of the Huron: How many weapons do they have?

Macapacelite: We counted three mortars, two six-pound cannon, and one three-pound cannon.

Pontiac: Approximately how many troops and other men would you estimate are present?

Macapacelite: There are about one hundred twenty soldiers and thirty-five English civilians who could help defend the fort.

Chief of the Potawatomi: Do not forget the two ships we saw anchored in the river. They also have soldiers on board, and they must have cannon as well.

Pontiac: Our only hope is to take the British without warning. Next week, we will visit the major again, only this time we will come armed.

Macapacelite: How can we enter the fort carrying weapons? The sentries will not let us through the gate if we are armed.

Pontiac: We will conceal our knives, hatchets, and guns under our blankets. Once inside, we will take the British by surprise when I give the sign. Go now and have your warriors file and saw off their muskets so they can be hidden easily.

Narrator 2: The chiefs leave to prepare their braves for battle.

Act III, Scene 4

Narrator 1: It is dawn on May 7, 1763. Pontiac has chosen this early hour to approach Fort Detroit because there is a chill in the air and the Indians will not look suspicious wearing blankets.

Major Gladwin has learned of Pontiac's conspiracy from a few Frenchmen who witnessed Indians sawing off their muskets. The Indians, in their excitement about going to war, made no attempt to conceal their preparations. The sentry on duty sends the French interpreter and some soldiers to meet Pontiac outside the entrance.

Pontiac: (*speaking to the interpreter*) I have come, as previously arranged, to visit with your commander.

Interpreter: Major Gladwin expects you. Please enter.

Narrator 2: Pontiac and his warriors, wrapped in blankets, walk into Fort Detroit. When they are all on the parade ground, the gate slams shut behind them and soldiers armed with rifles appear on the walls surrounding them. The fort's cannon also have been aimed at the Indians. Pontiac is furious when he realizes that he has been betrayed. He stalks up to Major Gladwin, who has come out onto his porch with some officers.

Gladwin: (sarcastically) Good morning, Chief Pontiac. Another mission of peace?

Narrator 2: Pontiac does little to hide his anger and points to the soldiers and cannon.

Pontiac: Why have you greeted us in this unfriendly manner? We have come to you in peace.

Gladwin: (pretending that nothing is wrong) I offer you gifts of bread and tobacco again in the hope that you will go in peace.

Narrator 2: Pontiac accepts the gifts. He and his confused warriors turn to leave. When Major Gladwin sees that there will be no immediate trouble, he signals the sentry to open the gate, and the Indians depart. When the Indians are a safe distance from the fort, Pontiac turns and speaks to his people.

Pontiac: We have been betrayed but not defeated. We will return and destroy Fort Detroit. Our brother tribes will attack all British outposts in the West and slay every Englishman they come across. We will win back our lands!

Narrator 2: Pontiac's warriors let out a war whoop and then return to their campsite. Back in the fort, Major Gladwin addresses his officers.

Gladwin: Prepare for war. Pontiac and his warriors will surely return and attack us.

Officer: Major Gladwin, there is a British soldier at the main gate with an urgent message for you.

Gladwin: Bring him to me at once.

Narrator 2: A disheveled soldier, covered with blood, approaches Major Gladwin.

Soldier: Sir, I have news for you from nearby Fort Sandusky. Hundreds of Ottawa and Huron Indians have besieged the fort and killed everyone except me. I was lucky to escape.

Gladwin: This does not surprise me. The gathering of the Indians a week and a half ago on the Ecorse River was a war council. I am thankful that the French spies warned us. We must prepare for a long siege.

Narrator 1: For several months, other segments of Pontiac's conspiracy are carried out. Various tribes destroy all the British forts in the western Great Lakes area except Fort Detroit. Major Gladwin's endurance and reinforcements from the East hold the fort. The British are determined not to surrender, and Pontiac begins to lose the confidence of his people. The Indians eventually abandon their effort and return to their homelands. They want to hunt before the winter months set in, and they are tired of a hopeless battle. The Indians now want to live in peace with the British, just as they have done with the French.

Pontiac's dream is destroyed. He accepts his defeat and returns to his village, no longer the great chief of all the Indians in the West. Three years later, Pontiac uses what little power he has left to get the Indians to sign a peace treaty with the British. In 1769, Pontiac is killed by a Peoria Indian for an unknown reason.

> *"We have been betrayed but not defeated. We will return and destroy Fort Detroit."*

Resource Activities

True or False?

1. Pontiac was the chief of all the Indians west of the Appalachian Mountains.
2. The Delaware Prophet sent for Pontiac to discuss the ouster of the British.
3. Pontiac learned from French traders that France would support him and his warriors in a war against the British.
4. Pontiac held his war council deep in the woods so as not to alert the British to his plans.
5. All the Indian tribes planned to stay with Pontiac until the British were routed.
6. Major Gladwin, commander of Fort Detroit, knew of Pontiac's secret meeting with the Indians on the banks of the Ecorse River.
7. Pontiac's plan to gain entrance into Fort Detroit called for his leading several Indians to the fort and asking permission to talk with the commander.
8. When Pontiac and his warriors returned to Fort Detroit, they were not allowed to enter.
9. Pontiac never revealed to the British that he and his men had come armed. Pontiac pretended he had come in peace and was hurt to see the British take up arms.
10. The other Indian tribes decided not to attack the other British forts after Pontiac's second entry into Fort Detroit failed.

Do You Remember?

1. Why was the support of the Delaware Prophet so important to Pontiac?
2. What was the main difference between the French presence and the British presence in the Great Lakes region and to the south?
3. Why did the Indian chiefs so readily agree to join Pontiac ?
4. Why did Pontiac want to perform a ceremonial dance for the British?

5. What was Pontiac's command to the Indians who did not accompany him to the fort for the ceremonial dance?
6. What was Pontiac's signal for the chiefs of the other tribes to begin attacking the British forts in their areas?
7. What did the British at Fort Detroit offer the Indians as a sign of their friendship?
8. How did Pontiac plan for his warriors to disguise their weapons on their return visit to Fort Detroit?
9. Did the Indians wait for Fort Detroit to be destroyed before they attacked other British forts?
10. Did Pontiac ever destroy Fort Detroit?

What Do You Think?

1. Would Pontiac have succeeded in uniting the Indian tribes if he had not had the support of the Delaware Prophet?
2. What did the dress and appearance of the Delaware Prophet tell Pontiac about his personality? What did the dress and appearance of Pontiac tell the Delaware Prophet about his personality?
3. The Great Spirit urged his people to return to the ways of their ancestors. He disliked how the Indians had adopted so many customs of the white people. List several factors that you think might have contributed to his feelings.
4. In general, why did the Indians prefer the French to the British at this time?
5. Why was surprise necessary in Indian warfare against the British?
6. Pontiac planned two visits to Fort Detroit. Was his first visit necessary? Was the first visit used only to spy on the British?
7. Why did Pontiac send his allies home to prepare for war? What might have been his reasons for not keeping them all together for a ground attack on Fort Detroit?

8. Why did Pontiac neglect to counsel his men to be secretive about preparing their weapons?

9. How did Major Gladwin handle Pontiac's second visit?

10. Why might the French spies have given information to the British about the Indians?

From the Historical Perspective

1. Interpreters are frequently used in negotiations between people who do not speak the same language. Are there any disadvantages to this method of negotiation? If so, explain.

2. The Proclamation Line of 1763 was drawn by the British. What was their intent? What was the colonists' reaction? Was the Proclamation Line realistic?

Further Activities

1. Research and compare other Indian chiefs, such as Massasoit, King Philip, Tecumseh, Chief Joseph, Chief Crazy Horse, and Sitting Bull.

2. Research the various lands set aside as Indian territories in the 1700s and 1800s. In the library, find the names of Indian reservations in existence today. Write for information. If possible, visit one. Inquire about writing to a pen pal.

3. Research how the English land companies sponsored colonies such as Jamestown, Plymouth, and Massachusetts Bay and how they planned to make money from them.

CHAPTER TWO

CHILDREN OF THE REVOLUTION

Historical Overview

British control of the American Colonies became increasingly harsh after the French and Indian War, which ended in 1763 with the Treaty of Paris. England sent additional troops to patrol the frontiers and enforce the Proclamation Line of 1763, which had been drawn to keep the colonists east of the Appalachian Mountains and the Indians west of the mountains. What aroused even more indignation was England's insistence that the colonists house and feed these troops.

England's leaders also felt that the colonists should be taxed to repay the huge debt caused by the war, since British soldiers had fought to protect the Colonies. In 1765, Parliament passed the Stamp Act. It decreed that all legal documents and other printed materials such as newspapers and playing cards carry a stamp to prove the tax had been paid on the item. There was great resistance to the Stamp Act throughout the Colonies. Patrick Henry, one of the more powerful and outspoken speakers in the Colonies, condemned the Stamp Act as taxation without representation during a speech in the Virginia Assembly. While many felt that he spoke too strongly, his speech was quickly printed and echoed throughout the Colonies.

Most colonists were law-abiding citizens, loyal to England and their king. They did not want war. Yet the constant passage of new acts of Parliament outraged them. Many people refused to pay the new taxes. People began smuggling goods into the Colonies to bypass paying taxes. They also organized boycotts. To curb such practices, the British imposed even more taxes, which increased the hardships for the colonists.

The colonists began to rethink their allegiance to England. Groups of men banded together under the name Sons of Liberty. They swore not to use any goods that were taxed and to stop drinking tea. Groups of women banded together under the name Daughters of Liberty. They wove their own cloth and refused to wear or use any imported cloth from England. Tall masts were set up with a cap or banner at the top to mark the meeting places of the Sons of Liberty. These masts came to be known as Liberty Poles.

As tempers flared and more protests occurred, incidents of burning and tarring and feathering were common. In 1770, a clash between colonists and British soldiers resulted in the deaths of four colonists. This became known as the Boston Massacre. Finally, under great pressure from British merchants who profited from Colonial trade, Parliament repealed many of the taxes—except the tax on tea.

In Massachusetts, Samuel Adams, a very outspoken patriot, decided to form a Committee of Correspondence. Its purpose was to inform the colonists through letters and pamphlets about British events that might create problems for them. Soon other colonies organized Committees of Correspondence. These committees provided a communication link and a unifying force among the colonies.

In 1773, the Committees of Correspondence circulated news that Parliament had passed the Tea Act. This law allowed a financially troubled British tea company to sell its product cheaply to the colonists. Colonial merchants were furious because only specially chosen stores were allowed

to sell the tea. The Sons of Liberty urged action. If England continued to follow this procedure with other items, Colonial merchants would soon be out of business. The result was the Boston Tea Party, in which a group of radical colonists dressed as Mohawk Indians dumped 342 chests of British tea into Boston Harbor. England retaliated against the colonists by passing more laws, especially against Massachusetts, which Parliament considered the ringleader. The port of Boston was closed to all shipping. The colonies reacted by sending twelve delegates (Georgia was not represented) to the First Continental Congress. The idea of freedom from England began to be considered, and Congress strongly advised each colony to set up and train its own militia.

Many colonists still hoped for a peaceful settlement. Most were farmers and trades-people who could not afford to spend time away from their families and business responsibilities. Many, while opposed to Parliament's acts, were still loyal to England and the king.

On April 19, 1775, the British met several contingents of American colonists on the battlefields of Lexington and Concord. The Second Continental Congress met in Philadelphia on May 10, 1775. All thirteen colonies were represented this time. The delegates unanimously elected George Washington as general and commander in chief of the Continental Army. While several delegates wanted to declare independence from England, most still hoped for a peaceful settlement.

Throughout the Colonies, cities and towns buzzed with the news of Lexington and Concord, overshadowing the other pressing problems of the time. Nowhere was this more evident than in the area north of Connecticut and west of the Connecticut River, in present-day Vermont. Land speculation had increased tremendously there after the Proclamation Line of 1763 was drawn. Benning Wentworth, the royal governor of New Hampshire, in his greed to amass money and land, had overstepped his bounds of authority and sold tracts of land in this territory, which also was claimed by New York. A bitter fight occurred when New York began enforcing its boundaries and demanded the retreat of Wentworth's purchasers, many of whom had settled and were farming the land.

Ethan Allen, a strong, self-confident, and self-reliant young man, offered to fight for those who claimed tracts of land in Vermont. His followers became known as the Green Mountain Boys. Angry discussions, confusing court sessions, and several illegal skirmishes followed. The case was still in court when Allen heard about Lexington and Concord. He quickly changed his priorities and decided to fight for the cause of freedom by planning an attack on Fort Ticonderoga. Capturing the fort, which was close to British-ruled Canada, would prevent the British from using it as a stopping point for their troops entering the American Colonies. Ticonderoga also had cannon and ammunition, both of which were in very short supply in the colonists' camps. Allen did not wait for orders or a charge from the Continental Congress. He saw an opportunity and took advantage of it.

Allen had his followers, but he still needed help. Other leaders throughout the Colonies also found they needed assistance to accomplish their aims. This help frequently came from children and teen-agers. The population of the American Colonies was young. Settlers were usually young adults. Many came with children or began families once they were settled. Children were expected to help with the chores from an early age. Schooling was not mandatory. As a result, children spent much time in the company of adults, listening to them discuss the rights and needs of the colonists. As the revolutionary spirit spread, people in all walks of life became involved. The children of the times also sought to do their part, however small, to further the cause of the new nation.

The roles children played during the American Revolution are often overlooked. The following three plays are based on true stories about the contributions some children made that influenced the course of American history.

Nathan Beman:
The Boy Who Led the Colonists Against Fort Ticonderoga

Characters

Ethan Allen — the commander of the Green Mountain Boys and the small army that seizes Fort Ticonderoga

Benedict Arnold — the captain of the Connecticut militia

Nathan Beman — the nine-year-old son of a local farmer

Master Beman — Nathan Beman's father

Mistress Beman — Nathan Beman's mother

Major Beach — a colonist who leads a band of volunteers

Captain Delaplace — Fort Ticonderoga's commandant

Lieutenant Feltham — the second in command at Fort Ticonderoga

Introduction

Narrator 1: In 1775, some American colonists thought that it would further their cause against the British to capture Fort Ticonderoga and seize the large quantity of military supplies stored there. Gunpowder and cannon were needed especially by the colonists around Boston. It also was rumored that the fort had fallen into disrepair, making it a good time to attack. Ethan Allen, commander of the expedition, and Benedict Arnold, his second in command, led their small army of two hundred thirty soldiers to the southern end of Lake Champlain. Surprise was necessary if they were to be victorious.

The soldiers at Fort Ticonderoga were not aware that they were about to be attacked. To catch the British off guard, the colonists had to cross the lake before sunrise. They also needed a guide to show them the layout of the fort.

Act I, Scene 1

Narrator 1: A hidden campsite at Hand's Cove on the southern shores of a narrow part of Lake Champlain, about one mile north of Fort Ticonderoga. It is May 9, 1775, and Ethan Allen and his small army of colonists have been hiding in the woods for a day waiting for boats to arrive to carry them across the lake to the fort. Allen also is trying to find a local person who can guide them into the fort once they arrive there. Allen and Benedict Arnold are sitting around a campfire because there is a chill in the early May air.

Ethan Allen: We need more men. Our forces are too small to take the fort, even by surprise.

Benedict Arnold: I have been expecting about fifty more recruits from New England. They must have lost their way.

Allen: And where are the boats I requested? We need several large bateaux to cross this narrow bit of water swiftly so we can attack the fort before dawn. If we do not get more cooperation from the locals, our mission will not succeed.

Arnold: A Master Beman from Shoreham is rounding up some boats and should be here with them soon.

Allen: What about a guide for when we get to the fort?

Arnold: Master Beman said that his son could help us.

Allen: His son! How old is the boy?

Arnold: I do not know. We shall find out when Master Beman returns with him and our boats.

Narrator 2: Several soldiers jump up from around their campfires as a large group of weary men stumble into the campsite.

Allen: *(looking up)* What is that commotion?

Arnold: It looks like Major Beach has just arrived.

Narrator 2: The major, wet, dirty, and very tired, appears in front of the two leaders.

Allen: *(impatiently)* Where have you been, Major? We have been waiting for reinforcements. We are outnumbered by the British garrison at the fort.

Major Beach: I have traveled sixty miles in twenty-four hours, and I have gathered together fifty Colonial volunteers to add to your forces.

Allen: Great! Now we are ready to attack the fort. You and your men must now rest. I plan to leave for the fort as soon as our boats arrive.

Narrator 2: The major leaves to catch

some sleep with his men.

Arnold: I will send a messenger to find Master Beman, our guide, and our boats.

Allen: It is embarrassing waiting here on the shore when we are so close to the enemy. I want to reach the fort before sunrise so we can surprise the British. We must leave tonight, or they will get word of our presence here.

Narrator 2: Arnold leaves to send one of his men to find Master Beman.

Act I , Scene 2

Narrator 1: The Beman farmhouse in Shoreham, a settlement about three miles east of Hand's Cove. Master and Mistress Beman are talking about the Colonial army that arrived the day before. They are anxious to help the colonists because they do not like the British.

Master Beman: I must return to the Continental Army's camp. I have had word that Colonel Allen is waiting for boats to ferry his men across the lake to the fort before sunrise tomorrow.

Mistress Beman: How many boats did you get?

Master Beman: Colonel Allen is going to be disappointed. I have been able to find only one bateau and a small boat.

Mistress Beman: How many men are there?

Master Beman: More than two hundred.

Mistress Beman: And you have only two boats? He certainly *is* going to be disappointed.

Master Beman: The bateau can carry many men. It will have to do. I must leave soon. Where is Nathan? He is to accompany me to the camp.

Mistress Beman: I know you said that

> *"Nathan has visited the British soldiers so many times that it is like a second home to him."*

Colonel Allen needs a guide, but why must it be our son? He is only nine years old.

Master Beman: Nathan knows the fort inside and out. He has visited the British soldiers so many times that it is like a second home to him. Besides, the soldiers will not harm him.

Mistress Beman: It will still be dangerous. He could be wounded by a stray bullet.

Master Beman: We must all take chances to help win our freedom. Call the boy so that we can leave.

Mistress Beman: He is in his room, but I am sure he has not been sleeping. He was so excited when you told him that he was to help Colonel Allen and his army. *(calling her son)* Nathan, your father is ready to leave.

Narrator 2: Nathan has been listening to his parents talk and is dressed and ready to go. He quickly climbs down the ladder from the loft and stands before his father.

Master Beman: Well, son, are you ready to help the Continental Army?

Nathan Beman: *(throwing back his shoulders and answering proudly)* Yes, sir.

Master Beman: We must leave immediately. Colonel Allen is anxious to cross the lake and get to the fort while it is still dark. You must show him where he can enter with his men unnoticed. They plan to take the fort by surprise.

Nathan: I am ready to help, Father. I know just the spot to show Colonel Allen.

Master Beman: You can tell him yourself soon.

Narrator 2: Mistress Beman hugs her son and husband good-bye. As they leave the farmhouse, Nathan bravely walks into the night with his father.

Mistress Beman: *(calling out to them with*

tears in her eyes) God be with you, Nathan, and with you, my husband.

Act I, Scene 3

Narrator 1: A hidden spot on the shore of Hand's Cove. The two boats have just arrived, and Ethan Allen and Benedict Arnold talk to Nathan Beman and his father as the men prepare to cross the lake. It is 2 A.M. on May 10, 1775, and in only three hours, the sun will begin to rise.

Allen: Master Beman, I need more than two boats. We have more than two hundred men to transport to the other side of this lake in three hours.

Master Beman: I expected to get several boats from a neighboring town, but there was not enough time to bring them here.

Allen: Then we have to rely on the two boats that you brought. We will fill them with as many men as we can. I will lead them to take the fort by surprise. Our first attack must be before the British awake and the sun betrays our location. Then the boats will return for the rest of the troops.

Arnold: That is the most sensible plan we can follow under the circumstances.

Allen: *(turning back to Master Beman)* Where is the young guide whom I have heard about? I will need him to show us the best way into the fort.

Narrator 2: Master Beman motions to Nathan, who has been standing in the background, to come forward. Nathan stands at attention in front of the famous commander of the Green Mountain Boys.

Master Beman: *(proudly)* Colonel Allen, this is my son, Nathan. He has agreed to

> *The sight of the boy bravely standing beside their leader gives the men the courage to move on and take the fort.*

help you gain access to the fort.

Allen: How old are you, son?

Nathan: *(standing up as tall as he can)* Almost ten, sir.

Allen: You are very brave to offer to go into battle with us. How is it that you know so much about Fort Ticonderoga?

Nathan: I have often rowed over to the fort and pretended to be a spy. The British let me come and go as I please, so I know the buildings inside as well as the area outside the walls.

Allen: Where do you suggest that we can enter the fort with the least chance of being seen?

Nathan: There is a breach in one of the outer walls on the south side that has never been repaired. We can go through there to a wicket gate that can be entered easily. The sentry on duty at that entrance is a careless man. He always lets me in without asking any questions.

Allen: Perfect! Once we are in the fort, can you lead me to the commandant's quarters?

Nathan: Yes, I know where that is.

Allen: Good. We will leave at once. *(turning to his second in command)* Colonel Arnold, you follow with the rest of our men when the boats return.

Narrator 1: Eighty-three men crowd into the two boats. Soon after, they land on the opposite shore about one mile north of Fort Ticonderoga just as the sun begins to rise. Nathan is at Allen's side as he makes a speech to the men preparing them for the imminent attack. Allen tells them how important it is to seize the fortress and its store of supplies. The sight of the boy bravely standing beside their leader gives the men the courage to move on and take the fort. They also have the reassurance that the boats have already returned to

Hand's Cove to pick up the rest of the army.

Act I, Scene 4

Narrator 1: The colonists have not been detected as they approach Fort Ticonderoga. Only a lonely sentry is on duty, and his poorly charged musket misfires when Allen and his men rush through the wicket gate. Once in the courtyard, Allen has his men point their muskets at the barracks filled with sleeping British soldiers.

Allen: Let us rouse the British out of their beds. Give me three cheers for the Continental Army!

Narrator 2: The men give three mighty cheers. As a result, Lieutenant Feltham, the second in command at the fort, and the soldiers jump out of their beds and stumble into the courtyard in their nightshirts, clutching their swords and muskets.

Allen: *(in a very loud voice)* I demand the surrender of this fort!

Lieutenant Feltham: In whose name do you make this demand?

Allen: In the name of the Great Jehovah and the Continental Congress!

Narrator 2: The lieutenant realizes that Allen is serious. He instructs his men to surrender their arms.

Allen: *(turning to Nathan)* Now, my friend, show me where the commandant's quarters are located.

Nathan: This way, sir.

Narrator 2: Nathan leads Allen into a building and up some stairs. As they approach the commandant's room, Captain William Delaplace, who has quickly dressed in his uniform, steps out onto the landing.

Captain Delaplace: What is all this commotion?

Allen: *(confronting the British commander)* I demand the surrender of this fort.

Narrator 2: The captain, looking down at his soldiers unarmed and surrounded by the American troops in the courtyard below, turns and quietly surrenders his sword. Allen accepts the sword and, with his arm around Nathan's shoulders, returns to the courtyard and his victorious army. They have won an important victory for the freedom of the Colonies.

Narrator 1: The loss of Fort Ticonderoga cost the British their pride as well as their valuable supplies. The fort was captured in ten minutes without a shot being fired or the loss of any life by a small army of volunteers led by a courageous commander and guided by a nine-year-old boy. If it had not been for the bravery of Nathan Beman, the course of American history might have been different. Certainly the fortress would not have been seized so easily and without bloodshed.

Three Young Patriots and the Liberty Pole

Characters

Polly Daggett — a young girl who lives on Martha's Vineyard
Parnel Manter — a young girl who lives on Martha's Vineyard
Maria Allen — a young girl who lives on Martha's Vineyard

Master Daggett — Polly's father and a town selectman
Mistress Daggett — Polly's mother

Introduction

Narrator 1: In 1776, the people of Martha's Vineyard tried to keep their island off the coast of Massachusetts officially neutral during the American Revolution. This was difficult, however, as their sympathies had been with the rebelling patriots since the British forced the Stamp Act on the American Colonies eleven years earlier.

The children of the island shared their parents' feelings. The loyalty of three teen-aged girls who lived in the village of Holme's Hole (now known as Vineyard Haven) was put to the test when the British demanded that their Liberty Pole be used to replace the broken mast of a British ship.

Act I, Scene 1

Narrator 1: The home of the Daggett family in Holme's Hole. It is dinner time. Master Daggett, a selectman (one of a board of officers elected to take care of public business), is telling his wife and daughter, Polly, the news of the day.

Master Daggett: Yesterday the British frigate *Unicorn* barely managed to sail into our harbor.

Polly Daggett: Father, what is a frigate?

Master Daggett: A small war vessel.

Mistress Daggett: What was wrong with it?

Master Daggett: One of its masts was broken during a violent storm when it was crossing the North Atlantic.

Polly: Why did it come to our island? We do not like the British here.

Master Daggett: Because Martha's Vineyard is supposed to be neutral in this war between England and the American Colonies.

Polly: (*angrily*) I do not like being labeled neutral. I am proud to call myself a patriot. How can we declare our neutrality to a country that forced the Stamp Act on the Colonies, caused the Boston Massacre, and passed a bill closing the port of Boston? I take the side of the "Indians" who threw the British tea into Boston Harbor.

Master Daggett: (*patiently*) Polly, we are very vulnerable because of our defenseless position as an island. We have been forced

to declare our neutrality. If we had not done so, the British would have attacked and defeated us.

Mistress Daggett: Did any of the sailors on the *Unicorn* come ashore?

Master Daggett: Yes, they searched the island all day yesterday for a tree of a suitable size to replace their ship's broken mast.

Polly: Did they find one?

Master Daggett: No, they did not find a tree. But they found a pole large enough for their use. The other village selectmen and I received a message from the captain this morning demanding that we sell them the pole we have on our hill.

Polly: *(her voice trembling)* Not the Liberty Pole?

Master Daggett: I am afraid so.

Polly: *(indignantly)* But they cannot have our Liberty Pole! We put it up last year as a symbol of our sympathy with the patriots on the mainland. Father, what did you tell the captain?

Master Daggett: At first we refused his request. Then the captain sent us a reply stating that if we would not sell the pole to him, he would consider it a rebellious act and destroy Holme's Hole. We had no choice but to comply with his wishes.

Mistress Daggett: Have they taken it yet?

Master Daggett: No, the captain informed us that he would send his men to get the pole tomorrow morning.

Polly: *(sadly)* I cannot believe that we will lose our beloved pole. I remember the excitement the day it was erected on Manter's Hill last year. Our entire village turned out for the event.

Mistress Daggett: Yes, the day was a joyous occasion.

Master Daggett: I also remember that day fondly. We all worked hard to put up the pole. After we carried it to the top of the hill, the other men and I dug a deep hole to secure the pole, and then we fastened several ropes to hoist it.

Polly: The other children and I tied flags of different colors to the pole, and they fluttered in the wind when you raised it. We all cheered and sang songs.

Mistress Daggett: We women threw tea into the hole before you filled it in. This was our way of protesting the tax on tea.

Polly: It was just like the time the Bostonians protested by dumping a whole shipload of tea into Boston Harbor. Father, how can you sell our Liberty Pole to the

British? It means so much to us.

Master Daggett: Do not forget, Polly, that many of our young men have enlisted in the Continental Army on the mainland. We are helpless in defending our island. Go and play with your friends and try to forget this unhappy moment.

Polly: Yes, Father, I will go to Maria Allen's house. But I will never forget what the British have done to us.

Narrator 2: Polly gets up from the dinner table, leaving her parents to continue their conversation. She heads for Maria Allen's house. As she runs along, she devises a plan. She stops to pick up another friend, Parnel Manter, and they both go to the Allen home. Polly is anxious to tell the two girls the news of the day. She also is determined to solicit their help with her plan to prevent the British from getting the Liberty Pole.

Act I, Scene 2

Narrator 1: Maria Allen's bedroom. Polly tells Parnel and Maria the news her father told her and her mother at dinner that evening. Parnel and Maria also are upset about selling the Liberty Pole to the British. They are eager to prevent this from happening, and they listen intently to Polly's plan.

Polly: We must destroy the Liberty Pole before the British take it away to use on their ship. This will be our contribution to the Revolution.

Parnel Manter: How will three girls ever do that? You said the British sailors are coming tomorrow morning to get the pole. That does not give us time to do much of anything.

Maria Allen: I cannot imagine how we can destroy such a huge pole.

Polly: We will blow up the Liberty Pole!

Maria and Parnel: (together) Blow it up! With what?

Polly: Leave that to me. Now listen carefully.

Narrator 2: The three girls move closer together so that Maria's parents cannot overhear their plans. They would certainly stop the girls from doing something so dangerous. Polly whispers her instructions.

Polly: Maria, your father must have a ship's auger [a tool for boring holes] in his shop.

Maria: I am sure he does. Why?

Polly: You must take it without being seen and bring it to the Liberty Pole in one hour.

Maria: (nervously) I will, but it will be dark by then.

Polly: Yes, and all the better for us. We will not be seen. (turning to Parnel) Parnel, can you bring a warming pan full of live coals to the hill?

Parnel: (puzzled) I think so. But whatever for? It is not that cold outside.

Polly: You will soon see why we need coals. Now let us go quietly and meet on Manter's Hill in one hour. And remember, we must not get caught. If we do, we will surely be severely punished and the British will have a new mast for their warship.

Narrator 2: The girls leave the house and quickly go about completing their assigned tasks. Polly returns to her house to borrow her father's powder horn and some gunpowder.

Act I, Scene 3

Narrator 1: The top of Manter's Hill. It is dark, and Polly, Parnel, and Maria arrive with the materials needed to accomplish their important mission.

Polly: Did either one of you have any trouble?

Maria: It was easy to get into my father's shop. No one was there. I just had to find his auger among all his tools. Here it is. *(holds up a ship's auger)*

Polly: Good, I hope it is sharp.

Maria: I am sure it is. My father takes good care of his tools.

Polly: Parnel, I see you have a warming pan. Are the coals hot?

Parnel: They are.

Maria: How did you manage to get it out of the house? You could hardly hide it under your cloak as I hid the auger.

Parnel: I told my mother I was chilled and needed some coals to warm up my bed. She looked at me strangely because I never go to bed early and am not usually cold. When I got to my room, I climbed out of the window. I almost dropped the pan when I landed on the ground.

Polly: We are ready to begin our work. First we must drill several deep holes in the base of the pole. Then we will fill them with gunpowder from my father's hunting horn.

Parnel: That is why you need the live coals— to light the gunpowder.

Polly: Right. Now let us begin drilling. The holes must be deep enough to hold a good amount of powder to blow the pole apart.

Narrator 2: The three girls take turns drilling the holes in the pole. It is awkward work because they are not used to using the auger.

Maria: That was harder than I thought it would be. Now what do we do?

Polly: I will fill the holes with gunpowder while the two of you tear your petticoats and wad the cloth tightly into each opening.

> *"Do not look back. When we get to our homes, we must not tell anyone about our mission."*

Narrator 2: The three girls quickly but carefully complete this next step.

Polly: Now I am going to ignite the wads with some hot coals. As soon as they begin to burn, run as fast as you can down the hill and straight home. Do not look back. When we get to our homes, we must not tell anyone about our mission. If our parents are questioned by the British, they can truthfully say that they know nothing of what has happened to the Liberty Pole.

Narrator 2: The girls run down the hill when the wads start burning. Shortly thereafter, the Liberty Pole explodes in a large burst of flames. The pole is blown to bits. The girls return to their homes and join their families and the rest of the villagers, who are all wondering what caused the loud noise.

Narrator 1: The next morning, everyone in the village is aware that the Liberty Pole has been destroyed, but no one except Polly, Parnel, and Maria knows who did it. The captain calls the village selectmen together and demands to know what has happened to his new mast. He soon realizes by the perplexed expressions on their faces that they have no idea who blew up the pole. They are all relieved when the captain and his men return to the *Unicorn* and sail slowly away to look for a new mast somewhere else.

Polly, Parnel, and Maria have made their secret contribution to the cause of liberty and independence for the American Colonies. They do not tell their families and friends about their brave deed until the Revolution is over. Their courage, however, will long be remembered. Today there is a bronze plaque in the town of Vineyard Haven commemorating their act of patriotism.

Peter Francisco: The Young Giant of the American Revolution

Characters

Peter Francisco — a boy from Europe who grows up in the American Colonies

Judge Anthony Winston — an American patriot and owner of the Hunting Tower plantation in Virginia

George Washington — the commander of the Continental Army

General "Mad" Anthony Wayne — a general in the Continental Army*

Lieutenant Gibbon — the leader of a unit at the battle of Stony Point

House Mistress — the mistress of the Prince George County Poor House

*General Wayne aquired his nickname because of his daring and adventurous behavior.

Introduction

Narrator 1: On June 23, 1765, a European ship sailed up the James River and anchored offshore at City Point (now Hopewell) in southern Virginia. A longboat was lowered from the ship, and two sailors rowed to the nearest wharf, where they left a five-year-old boy. The boat returned to the ship, which immediately weighed anchor and sailed away back down the river, never to be seen again.

The abandoned child did not speak English, and the local people did not understand his language. They noticed, however, that he had the initials P.F. engraved on the silver buckles on his shoes, and he kept saying the name Pedro Francisco over and over again. They called him Peter Francisco.

Peter was a good-looking boy with a dark complexion, black hair, and dark, alert eyes. He appeared to be of Italian, Portuguese, or Spanish descent. Although his clothes were dirty and rumpled from his long journey across the Atlantic Ocean, they were obviously of good quality, with an expensive lace collar and cuffs. It was evident that he came from a family of some wealth.

The people of City Point felt sorry for Peter. They found an unused bed for him in a nearby warehouse. The local housewives fed him, and the watchman on the docks looked after him. A while later, the child was taken to the Prince George County Poor House, where he stayed until he was discovered by Judge Anthony Winston, a prominent and respected planter from Buckingham County, Virginia.

Act I, Scene 1

Narrator 1: As soon as Judge Anthony Winston arrives in City Point on business, he hears the story of the young foreign boy, Peter Francisco, who was abandoned at the dock several months earlier. Since his arrival, Peter has learned to speak enough English to tell what he can remember of his family and home. The judge is curious about the boy, and he visits him in the Prince George County Poor House. Peter is brought to the judge by the head mistress of the Poor House. The judge kneels down so that he can speak to Peter face to face.

> *The abandoned child did not speak English, and the local people did not understand his language.*

Judge Anthony Winston: What is your name, young man?

Peter Francisco: *(looking the judge directly in the eye and answering him)* Pedro Francisco.

Judge: Do you remember your home?

Peter: A little bit, sir.

Judge: Tell me about it.

Peter: It was a beautiful house near the ocean surrounded by gardens with many flowers and a gate opening onto the street. I remember that it was always sunny, with a warm breeze blowing off the ocean.

Judge: Can you recall your family?

Peter: *(tears fill his eyes as he remembers his mother)* My mother was small, with tan skin like mine. She was very pretty and kind. She usually spoke French.

Judge: *(kindly)* And your father?

Peter: He was tall, also with tan skin, and very stern. He was away a lot, and he spoke another language.

Judge: Did you have any brothers and sisters?

Peter: *(again with tears in his eyes)* I had a little sister.

Judge: *(softly)* You must have loved her very much.

Peter: I did.

Judge: How did you end up on a ship

that came to the American Colonies?

Peter: One day I was playing with my sister in our garden when two sailors came to our gate with candy and called to us. When we went over to see what they wanted, they unbolted the gate and grabbed us.

Judge: What happened to your sister?

Peter: She kicked and screamed so much that she escaped from their grasp. They threw a blanket over me, carried me to the ship, and sailed away. *(fighting back tears)* That was the last time I saw my home and family.

Judge: *(thinking for a minute)* You are a very brave little boy, and I like your quiet dignity. How would you like to come home with me and live on my plantation? You could go riding, hunting, and fishing on my many acres of farmland, woods, and streams. I have four children who are older, but I am sure they will like you. It is the ideal place for a boy to grow up. When you are old enough, you can help on the plantation.

Peter: I would like that, sir.

Judge: Then we will leave at once. *(turning to the Poor House mistress)* I will make the proper arrangements with the authorities.

House Mistress: Yes, sir. You are kind to give Peter a home.

Narrator 2: The judge instructs his servant to bring Peter with them. They soon leave for Hunting Tower plantation.

Act I, Scene 2

Narrator 1: Judge Winston's library at Hunting Tower. It is December 1776, and Peter is fifteen years old. He has lived with Judge and Mrs. Winston and their four children for almost eleven years. Peter has grown into a strong young man standing six feet six inches tall and weighing two hundred sixty pounds.

Peter has been greatly influenced by Colonial patriots such as Patrick Henry, a nephew of the judge who often visits the Winstons. He has developed a strong loyalty to his adopted country over the years. Peter is now standing before the judge.

Judge: Peter, you wanted to speak with me?

Peter: Yes, sir. I have come to ask your permission to join the Continental Army.

Judge: You asked me that a year ago after you attended the Virginia Convention with me. I told you to wait a year. As I remember, you were fired up by a speech my nephew Patrick Henry made to all the delegates.

Peter: Yes, sir. I was fired up. For years I have heard Patrick discuss in this very room the issues and complaints between the Colonies and England, but never have I heard him speak as he did that day. I have memorized the last few lines of that speech: "Is life so dear, or peace so sweet, as to be purchased at the price of chains and slavery? Forbid it Almighty God! I know not what course others may take, but, as for me, give me liberty, or give me death!"

Judge: Well said, lad. I, too, was impressed by those words. Are you sure that this is what you want? You may have the body of a man—a giant, I think—but you are still young.

Peter: *(holding himself with dignity)* I want to serve my adopted country where I have been so happy. Patrick was appointed colonel of the First Virginia Regiment, and I want to follow in his footsteps.

Judge: Peter, I gave you my word, and I will keep it. I will miss you, but I respect your reasons for leaving. I release you from

> *"They threw a blanket over me, carried me to the ship, and sailed away. That was the last time I saw my home."*

your bondage here at Hunting Tower. Your strength, courage, and level head will make you a good soldier. May God be with you.

Narrator 2: Peter enlists in the Tenth Virginia Regiment of the Continental Army under the command of Colonel Hugh Woodson. He is immediately sent for his basic training to Middlebrook, New Jersey.

Within a year, Peter establishes a reputation for bravery and being cool-headed. On September 11, 1777, at Shady Hollow Gap, he faces his first battle, where he stands his ground for forty-five minutes. This act of courage inspires other soldiers to do the same, enabling General George Washington to make an orderly retreat. Peter is wounded in the leg and is hospitalized with the Marquis de Lafayette, a Frenchman who has come to help the Colonials. Peter and Lafayette become great friends.

Act I, Scene 3

Narrator 1: The American colonists need a victory to boost the morale of the Continental Army, and it is decided to attack the well-fortified British fort at Stony Point. General Washington has appointed General "Mad" Anthony Wayne to lead the attack. General Washington gives General Wayne detailed instructions for this important assault in his headquarters.

George Washington: General Wayne, I want you to command the army that is going to win this battle for the Colonies. We must raise the spirits of the patriots and our army by a tremendous victory over the British.

General "Mad" Anthony Wayne: I will be honored, sir. What are your instructions?

Washington: Since most attacks occur right before dawn, you should surprise the British and storm the fort just after midnight. A dark and rainy night would be best.

Wayne: I cannot do much about the weather.

Washington: Keep all information from your men, except the officers, of course, until the moment before you begin your assault. That way there is little chance of any deserter betraying you.

Wayne: That is a good idea.

Washington: Agree on a password and have all your men wear something white so they will be distinguishable from the enemy at night.

Wayne: That is easily done.

Washington: Your army will be chosen from the light infantry. We are fortunate to have this elite volunteer unit that is always first into action. I will personally choose these commandos. I want to be sure that Peter Francisco is one of them. Not only has he proven to be a brave and competent soldier, but he also sets a good example for the other soldiers. Morale is always higher with Peter around. The men seem to gain confidence from him.

Wayne: He is young.

Washington: That is one of his advantages. The older soldiers do not want to be shown up by him.

Wayne: I will be glad to have his great strength. He is strong enough to lift a cannon.

Washington: So I have heard. Begin preparations at once. You cannot go wrong with young Peter on your side.

Narrator 2: Wayne leaves to carry out his orders.

Act I, Scene 4

Narrator 1: Stony Point at the camp of the Continental Army on July 15, 1779.

General Wayne is instructing the twenty-member unit that includes Peter before they go into battle that night. The nearby British fortress is located on the top of a steep rock formation. It is well fortified with many cannon and walls of defense.

Wayne: You men have been chosen to lead the advance. Lieutenant Gibbon will be your commanding officer. I have issued strict orders that this is to be a secret and quiet campaign. All dogs in the area have been killed so there will not be any barking at night when we begin the assault. Your muskets are to be unloaded but with your bayonets attached.

Lieutenant Gibbon: What about civilians in the area?

Wayne: They are being stopped and detained until we return.

Gibbon: Yes, sir.

Wayne: *(turning to Peter, who towers over the other soldiers)* Peter, pass out this white paper. All of you must put a piece in your hat so that you can recognize each other in the dark.

Peter: Yes, sir.

Wayne: Peter, I am going to give you and Lieutenant Gibbon a password to share with the men when the assault begins. That way there will be no mistaking anyone in the dark.

Peter: You can trust me, sir.

Wayne: This battle is important to the American Colonies. We need a victory. I am offering a reward of $500 and a promotion to the first soldier who gets into the fort, $400 to the second, $300 to the third, $200 for the fourth, and $100 to the fifth.

Narrator 2: The soldiers are impressed with the amount of money. Peter is determined to be one of the first soldiers to enter the fort.

Peter: I am anxious to begin. When do we leave, sir?

Wayne: Go and rest, Peter. You will be called to line up at eight o'clock. At 11:30 P.M., everyone will move forward. I want the assault to proceed just after midnight.

Narrator 2: The men, restless and excited, go to their tents to try to get some sleep.

Narrator 1: Peter and his fellow soldiers, armed with their bayonets and axes, quickly cut a path through the two lines of defense at the bottom of the hill and advance up the steep rocks to the fortress. Lieutenant Gibbon is first to climb over the fort's wall. Peter is second.

Peter receives a nine-inch wound in his stomach but still manages to kill three British soldiers. Even though he is badly wounded, he holds on to the flag staff all night and delivers it in the morning, increasing his reputation for courage throughout the army. Seventeen out of the twenty soldiers in the advance unit are killed in this battle. Peter is sent to Fishkill, New York, to recover from his wound, but soon he is back in action, for nothing can hold the young man down.

Word eventually gets back to General Washington that Peter has complained that his sword is like a toothpick. Washington personally orders a six-foot-long broadsword with a five-foot blade to be forged for the young man. The heaviest in the army, the sword is delivered to Peter on March 13, 1781, just before the Battle of Guilford Court House, where he puts it to good use against the British.

Peter Francisco's fame increases as he continues performing his incredible feats throughout the Colonies. Many years later, people continue talking and writing about the giant from Virginia who grew up with his adopted country as a child of the Revolution.

Resource Activities

True or False?

Nathan Beman

1. Ethan Allen wanted to attack Fort Ticonderoga under cover of darkness, just before dawn.
2. Master Beman was able to supply Allen with several boats.
3. Allen was able to transport all his men across to Fort Ticonderoga in one trip.
4. Nathan Beman was ready and willing to help Allen.

Liberty Pole

5. The selectmen on the island of Martha's Vineyard voted to support the patriots in the Revolutionary War.
6. The British captain of the *Unicorn* came ashore alone to ask islanders for a replacement for his mast.
7. The people of Martha's Vineyard set up a Liberty Pole to show their support for the Revolutionary cause.

Peter Francisco

8. Peter Francisco's parents sent him to the American Colonies.
9. Judge Anthony Winston encouraged and advised Peter to join the Continental Army.
10. General George Washington had a special sword made for Peter.

Do You Remember?

Nathan Beman

1. Where was Fort Ticonderoga located?
2. Who was Benedict Arnold?
3. Why did Nathan Beman, a young Colonial boy, know Fort Ticonderoga so well?
4. Who was in command of Fort Ticonderoga?

Liberty Pole

5. What did the women of Martha's Vineyard do to show their opposition to British laws?
6. Who brought the auger to the Liberty Pole, and why was it needed?
7. Why did Polly Daggett need hot coals to carry out her plan?

Peter Francisco

8. How did Peter Francisco's sister manage to escape her kidnappers?
9. What famous phrase did Patrick Henry use to end his protest against British-imposed taxes on the Colonies?
10. What did General George Washington advise General "Mad" Anthony Wayne to do so his men would recognize each other in battle?

What Do You Think?

Nathan Beman

1. Why did the colonists lack ammunition and cannon?
2. Why did the British allow Nathan Beman so much freedom in their fort?
3. What does Master Beman's attitude toward his son's involvement in the attack tell you about the colonists' attitude at the time?
4. When Ethan Allen found out he had only two boats, why did he not postpone his attack?

Liberty Pole

5. Why did Polly, Parnel, and Maria keep their secret about the Liberty Pole until after the Revolution?
6. Would Polly's plan have been as effective if she and her friends had been adults?
7. Was Martha's Vineyard's neutral position in the best interest of the Revolutionary cause?

Peter Francisco

8. What thoughts could Judge Anthony Winston have been thinking that made him so willing to take Peter Francisco home the first time he met him?

9. Why were the rewards for the soldiers who entered the enemy's fort first so high?

10. Why did General "Mad" Anthony Wayne order that the muskets be unloaded in the attack against Stony Point?

From the Historical Perspective

Nathan Beman

1. Why was Fort Ticonderoga important geographically?

Liberty Pole

2. Why were Liberty Poles, Committees of Correspondence, and groups such as the Sons of Liberty important?

Peter Francisco

3. Why were the strategies of night attacks and surprise attacks used so often by the colonists?

Further Activities

Nathan Beman

1. Benedict Arnold's name is synonymous in American history with the word "traitor." Find out why he changed his position after he helped capture Fort Ticonderoga.

Liberty Pole

2. Martha's Vineyard's position as an island made a defense against the British quite difficult. Find out how Nantucket and other islands, including Long Island, handled the situation.

Peter Francisco

3. The soldiers rallied around Peter Francisco. His courage inspired them. Generals liked to have him in their regiments. Think of some situation you may have read or seen, famous or ordinary, in which a young person spurred others on to action.

CHAPTER THREE

WOMEN OF THE REVOLUTION

Historical Overview

The 1770s were difficult times in the American Colonies. Breaking away from England was not an easy task. Not all colonists wanted to be free of English rule. Many tried to remain neutral, while others, especially merchants and those involved in professions such as law, medicine, and the church, remained loyal to England and the king. Even when Britain tried to strengthen its control and force the colonists into obeying British laws, all the colonists did not rebel.

When the First Continental Congress met in 1774, the purpose was clear: to mend the growing quarrel between the Colonies and England. The colonists wanted England to correct its wrongs and treat them as British subjects, not as a conquered people. Then came Lexington and Concord and the first battles between British soldiers and colonists.

When the Second Continental Congress met in Philadelphia in 1775, many representatives still advocated a peaceful settlement to the crisis. Their insistence on preserving peace, however, was less intense. The Second Continental Congress approved the formation of a Continental Army and appointed Virginian George Washington as commander. Britain reacted by sending twenty-five thousand additional soldiers to

crush the rebels.

On July 4, 1776, the Declaration of Independence was signed, with the patriots cheering the decision. Parliament vowed to defeat the rebels. Many colonists watched with great anxiety and wondered which side to join. But choices had to be made. Patriots had to take special care. Anyone who spied on or passed information about British troop formations and strategy was subject to arrest. Treason was punishable by death. On the other hand, Loyalists and Tories, the names given to those who favored the British, were not safe either. Colonists who wanted independence harassed Loyalists and Tories and often damaged or destroyed their property and possessions. They even tarred and feathered several unfortunate defenders of the Crown. In addition, it was difficult to know who was a Tory and who was a patriot, as some colonists changed sides depending on the situation or the turn of events.

The British had an effective undercover intelligence system working well before 1776. Their agents kept British officers in both the Colonies and England well informed about the pre-Revolutionary struggles and preparations. The Colonial intelligence system began with the Revolution. George Washington was at the center of most intelligence operations and controlled much of the spy network with the help of trusted friends and patriots. Smaller spy groups, such as that organized by the Darragh family in Philadelphia, were especially effective, since many of these operated in areas under British control.

Philadelphia was important to both the British and the colonists. The city was the center of the Colonies. Both Continental Congresses had met there, and the Declaration of Independence had been signed there. Yet because of its prominence and prosperity, many of its inhabitants were British subjects. British general Lord Howe knew this and marched his troops toward the city. In September 1777, he captured Philadelphia and made it his headquarters.

The colonists were disheartened at this turn of events but not discouraged. Their efforts now had to be better planned, since their central meeting point had been eliminated. To the colonists' advantage, General Howe was not one to act quickly. When his surprise assault on Whitemarsh,

just outside of Philadelphia and not far from Valley Forge where General Washington was encamped, failed to achieve results, Howe abandoned all other moves during the winter of 1777.

Activity to the north and south of Philadelphia continued. The British and the patriots constantly planned new strategies and surprise attacks. Many times their attempts failed due to increased spying and elaborate methods of relaying secret messages.

Each colony had its volunteer militia, composed of men divided into groups by area. These men were ready at a moment's notice to assemble and fight the enemy. Each unit had its commander, a person whom all could trust and respect. Colonel Ludington was one such commander. When George Washington was told that the colonel's daughter had ridden miles at night to summon the men in her father's unit against an advancing British column, the general traveled to the Ludingtons' farm and personally thanked the sixteen-year-old girl.

Colonial cities, ports, and commercial centers were most affected by the war. The frontier, however, was not quiet. The British asked the Indians to help them. Many agreed to such maneuvers because they sought to control the flood of settlers crossing into their territory and claiming their lands. White men, who had grown up along the frontier and had become trusted friends of the Indians, often led bands of Indians against the Colonial settlers. In addition, forts built along the frontier no longer provided safety and protection for those in the area. Since soldiers and ammunition were in short supply throughout the Colonies, those on the battlefronts received the first rounds and the frontier outposts received what could be spared.

The roles women played during the American Revolution are often overlooked when studying our country's history. The following three plays are based on true stories about the contributions three women made that influenced the course of American history.

The All-Night Ride of Sybil Ludington

Characters

Sybil Ludington — a sixteen-year-old girl who lives in New York

Colonel Henry Ludington — Sybil's father, a well-to-do farmer and the colonel of the Dutchess Seventh Militia of New York

Abigail Ludington — Sybil's mother

Courier — a messenger from the Continental Army

Introduction

Narrator 1: The American Revolution is in its second year. Colonel Henry Ludington is the commander of the Dutchess Seventh Militia of New York, the only Continental Army regiment between Danbury, Connecticut, and Peekskill, New York.

The Ludington family is widely known for its loyalty to the patriots and to the freedom of the American Colonies. Colonel Ludington fought in the French and Indian War and was recently the commissioner of public safety, being responsible for dealing with any Tories in his county. He is held in contempt by the British. It is rumored that British general Lord Howe has offered a large reward for his capture.

There is tension in the air as the Ludington family sits down to dinner on the evening of April 26, 1777. In the east toward the town of Danbury, the sky glows a crimson color. They suspect that the town is on fire, most likely the result of a British attack.

Colonel Ludington tries to make the meal a cheery one for his wife and eight children because he is sure that he will soon be called to battle. He brings up a subject dear to the hearts of all the children—their new yearling. There has been talk of selling the horse, but the children try their best to convince their father to keep it, especially the oldest, sixteen-year-old Sybil, who loves to ride. Henry Ludington welcomes this dicussion, for it distracts them all from the inevitable danger lurking on the horizon.

Colonel Henry Ludington: How has the yearling been progressing? Is he ready to be sold yet? *(grinning)* You must be tired of taking care of him.

> *"How could you manage to ride thirty miles from farmhouse to farmhouse in the dark of night?"*

Sybil Ludington: Father, you know how much I love taking care of your horses. Can you let me keep the yearling to ride?

Colonel Ludington: *(thinking over his answer and speaking slowly)* I do not know, Sybil. Because of the war, all horses are needed for the soldiers and to pull supply wagons and cannon.

Sybil: We all love the yearling, Father.

Colonel Ludington: To keep a horse just for pleasure does not seem right during these trying times.

Abigail Ludington: Sybil often rides the yearling on errands for me. That is not for pleasure.

Colonel Ludington: *(realizing he is outnumbered)* I will think this matter over. You do need a good, fast horse around the farm, especially with me gone so often.

Narrator 2: The Ludington children all cheer because they know they have won over their father. Suddenly they hear a horse come galloping into their yard. It stops in front of their house. Soon there is a loud knocking at the door.

Courier: Colonel Ludington! Colonel Ludington!

Narrator 2: Colonel Ludington jumps up from the table and runs to the door. He lets in an exhausted courier from the Continental Army.

Colonel Ludington: What can I do for you?

Courier: *(trying to catch his breath)* The British have made a surprise attack on Danbury and are now burning the town. They have captured the provisions from the Continental Army's storehouses.

Colonel Ludington: We saw the crimson glow in the sky. This is a great loss to us. There were valuable stores of food and am-

munition there. Who is their commander?

Courier: General William Tryon.

Colonel Ludington: How many troops does he have?

Courier: At least two thousand men.

Abigail: *(to her husband)* Were the storehouses not guarded by our soldiers?

Colonel Ludington: We left only one hundred fifty militiamen there to guard them. The rest of the soldiers were allowed to go home to their farms for spring plowing and planting. *(turning back to the courier)* Do you know where the British are going next?

Courier: They are headed for Ridgefield.

Colonel Ludington: The soldiers of the Dutchess Seventh Militia must be recalled from their farms immediately. The spring crops will have to wait. We must stop the British. My men and I will leave by dawn. *(to the courier)* You cannot gather my regiment tonight. You and your horse are exhausted and should not travel any farther.

Courier: *(trying to pull himself together)* I could try, sir.

Colonel Ludington: No, lad. You have done enough already just getting word to me. *(turning to his wife)* Abigail, give this young man some food and drink. He deserves to eat and rest so that he will be able to ride with us at sunrise.

Abigail: Certainly. I have some hot stew left from dinner.

Colonel Ludington: *(to Sybil, who has returned from putting the frightened younger children to bed)* Sybil, will you and your brother tend to this young man's horse? He should be groomed and fed. We will need him in the morning when we leave to stop the British. I must find someone to call up my men. They are scattered over thirty miles of countryside. I cannot go because I have to be here to organize the men as they arrive.

Sybil: *(excitedly)* I can go, Father.

Colonel Ludington: You are only sixteen years old. How could you manage to ride thirty miles from farmhouse to farmhouse in the dark of night?

Sybil: I could ride the yearling, and I know where all the farms are.

Colonel Ludington: The yearling is not

even completely broken in yet.

Sybil: But Mother told you that I have already ridden him on errands. He is fast and very sure of foot. Your men have to be warned, and there is no one else to do it.

Abigail: It is not the yearling's ability on the road or your skill as a rider that is our concern. There are Tories, deserters, and outlaws roaming around the countryside, especially at night. They are often desperate and dangerous. You will be alone.

Sybil: I will be careful. I promise. They will not be able to catch me.

Abigail: *(to her husband)* She is right, Henry. There is no one else to ride and alert all your men. If she promises to be careful, we must trust that she will be safe and successful. *(turning to her daughter)* Come with me. You will need a heavy woolen cloak to protect you from the cold spring wind and rain.

Colonel Ludington: I guess you are both right. We have no choice. You are a brave girl, Sybil, and I am proud of you for volunteering. I will get the yearling ready for your journey while you get dressed. Meet me in the yard. I will give you directions then.

Narrator 2: Colonel Ludington leaves to put a bridle and saddle on the yearling. A few minutes later, Abigail and Sybil appear in front of the barn. Mrs. Ludington hugs and kisses Sybil, and Colonel Ludington helps his daughter onto the horse.

Colonel Ludington: I will tell you the best route to take. First go south by the river to Carmel, then take Horse Pound Road to Lake Makopac. Then go to Tompkins Corner and turn right to Red Mills. Finally, ride north to Stormville, go through Peckville, and return home. Can you remember all that?

Sybil: Yes, Father. I will repeat it for you. *(repeats her father's directions)*

Colonel Ludington: Tell the men to meet me here before dawn. Warn the women that they should gather their valuables and prepare their children to be ready to leave in an instant if General Tryon appears to be coming this far.

Sybil: Yes, Father. You can trust me to carry out your orders.

Colonel Ludington: *(with worry and pride in his voice)* I know I can, Sybil. Godspeed!

Narrator 2: Sybil gallops off and is soon swallowed up by the darkness. Twenty minutes later, she reaches the first farmhouse. When the lights come on, Sybil calls out without dismounting.

Sybil: I am Colonel Ludington's daughter. I have come to alert you. The British have burned Danbury and are heading for Ridgefield. All men of the Dutchess Seventh Militia are to report to the Ludington farm immediately. Women and children must be prepared to flee with their valuables if the Redcoats come this far.

Narrator 2: When she finishes her message, Sybil continues her ride to all the farmhouses and villages in the area. At some houses, the lights do not go on. But all Sybil has to do is tell the inhabitants to look at the glowing sky in the east, and the frightened people jump out of bed. She does not reach every single house but knows that the word will spread to those she misses.

Twice when Sybil hears other riders on the road, she pulls over to the side to let them pass by. She is not about to take any chances, with Tories, deserters, and outlaws about.

Exhausted and splattered with mud, Sybil reaches her last stop at Peckville. She can barely repeat her message because her voice is hoarse from shouting her warning all night.

Dawn is breaking when Sybil and the weary yearling return to the Ludington farm. She is relieved when she sees hundreds of men preparing to march against the British. Her ride has been successful.

Narrator 1: The Dutchess Seventh Militia of New York was able to join the Connecticut militia in time to stop General Tryon at Ridgefield on April 27, 1777, and the British retreated to their ships in Long Island Sound. This was another victory of the American Revolution made possible because of the courage of a young woman.

Lydia Darragh:
The Quaker City Spy

Characters

Lydia Darragh — a respectable Quaker matron from Philadelphia

William Darragh — Lydia's husband

General William Howe — the British general head-

quartered in Philadelphia

British Officer — a member of General Howe's staff

Colonel Craig — a friend of the Darragh family and officer in the Continental Army

Introduction

Narrator 1: During the American Revolution, many colonists acted courageously as spies. They provided valuable military intelligence to the Continental Army and General George Washington. One such volunteer spy was the brave and clever Lydia Darragh, a Quaker from Philadelphia.

Lydia and her family lived in Loxley House at 177 Second Street, opposite Cadwalader House—the headquarters of British general Sir William Howe and later of Lieutenant General von Knyphausen. The location let Lydia observe the movements of the enemy staff every day. She even had the nerve, on occasion, to visit the headquarters and talk with some of the officers.

Lydia and her husband, William, usually worked together running an espionage operation from Loxley House. She collected information about the enemy's comings and goings and her conversations with them. Then William wrote her reports in shorthand on small pieces of paper. These were hidden in large buttons, which were covered with cloth and worn on coats. Whenever Lydia had any important military intelligence to give to General Washington, she would send her fourteen-year-old son, John, to the Continental Army's camp wearing the buttons. He would deliver them to his twenty-year-old brother, Lieutenant Charles Darragh, who had abandoned the Quaker belief of pacifism and joined the army. Charles, who could read shorthand, would translate the reports and pass the information on to General Washington.

Lydia performed this dangerous duty for her country for some time without being discovered. She did, however, have one

very close call. The British needed more rooms for their operations and ordered the Darragh family to give them their house. They had the right to seize the Darragh home because of an act of Parliament requiring American colonists to house and feed British troops. Lydia and her husband protested because they did not want to lose their source of espionage information. Compromising, the British agreed to use only one room. Lydia then sent her younger children to a home in the country for safety. Having the British meeting in their house gave the Darraghs access to more information. But their proximity to the action also made them more suspect when it was discovered that a secret had leaked out.

Act I, Scene 1

Narrator 1: Loxley House, the home of the Darragh family. Lydia Darragh has been instructed by the British to send her family to bed early on the evening of December 2, 1777, so that their officers can use the upstairs back room without interruption. The officers attending this secret conference will arrive at seven o'clock. Lydia is pleased at the prospect of having the opportunity to eavesdrop for more information to send to General Washington. She also is nervous about the risk she will be taking. She does not realize at this time that other American spies have already warned the Continental Army that the British are planning to surprise Washington at Whitemarsh. As the hall clock chimes seven times, there is a loud knock at the front door. Lydia, in her nightgown and holding a candle, opens the door. Several British officers step into the front hallway.

General William Howe: *(taking off his hat)* Good evening, Friend Darragh.

Lydia Darragh: *(curtsying)* Good evening, General.

Howe: I trust you received instructions to send all your family to bed early this evening.

Lydia: Yes, sir, I did. My husband and the older children are already in bed. I have been waiting for your arrival so I could let you in before I also retire.

British Officer: Where are your younger children?

Lydia: I have sent them to stay with relatives in the country. My husband and I do not think it appropriate to have young children around when our house is being used by you and your staff.

Howe: A good idea. We do not want to be interrupted tonight. Now please take us to our room.

Narrator 2: Lydia leads the British officers upstairs to the back room where the conference is to take place. She then obediently goes to bed herself. But she cannot sleep. Because of the secrecy involved, this is obviously an important meeting. As she hears the voices of the officers in the back room, she thinks of her son Charles who is lying asleep less than twenty-four miles away in the camp of the Continental Army at Whitemarsh. Are they plotting to attack her son's camp?

Lydia can stay in bed no longer. She must listen to their conversation. Maybe she can help General Washington again, or even save her son's life. Lydia steps out of bed and tiptoes into a closet adjoining the back room. In the closet, she overhears the word "Whitemarsh" and gasps out loud. The back room suddenly becomes quiet. But the British officers did not hear her.

> *She overhears the word Whitemarsh and gasps out loud. The back room suddenly becomes quiet.*

They only paused to look at a map of the area between Philadelphia and Whitemarsh. Relieved, Lydia presses her ear to the wall to listen to their plans.

Howe: This is our final decision. We will march out of Philadelphia early on the night of December 4. Our well-equipped army will make a surprise attack on Washington's army. We must keep this date a secret so the Americans will be unprepared. Have all the precautions been taken?

British Officer: Yes, sir. I am sure the Quaker woman can be trusted. Her people are against warfare, and she has always cooperated with us.

Howe: Make certain that she is asleep. We cannot afford to take any chances. Secrecy is crucial if this attack is to be a surprise.

Narrator 2: Chairs scrape the floor and swords rattle as the British officers rise from the table to leave. Lydia quickly creeps out of the closet and returns to her bedroom. One British officer stops by her door on his way out of the house. He speaks softly so as not to awaken the rest of the household.

British Officer: Friend Darragh.

Narrator 2: Lydia keeps quiet, pretending to be sound asleep.

British Officer: *(repeating himself, only louder)* Friend Darragh!

Narrator 2: Lydia, determined to convince the officer that she has been sound asleep, still says nothing. The British officer then knocks on the door. Lydia finally responds in a sleepy voice.

Lydia: Yes, who is there?

British Officer: I apologize for waking you, but I wanted you to know that we are leaving so you could lock the door behind us.

Lydia: Thank you. I shall.

Narrator 2: The British officers leave, satisfied that Lydia has been asleep. After locking the door, Lydia lies in bed planning how she can notify General Washington of the date of the surprise attack. She realizes that the life of her son and the lives of many other American men are in danger.

Act I, Scene 2

Narrator 1: The dining room of the Darraghs' home the next morning. During breakfast, Lydia gives her husband and children her itinerary for the day. She does not inform them, however, of her secret. If her family is questioned by the British, she wants them to be able to answer truthfully that they know nothing of the British plans. Besides, Lydia wants to warn General Washington herself. She also is afraid that if her husband knew her secret, he would not let her go on this very dangerous mission.

Lydia realizes that the life of her son and the lives of many other American men are in danger.

William Darragh: *(to his wife)* Did the British officers meet for a long time? I was so sound asleep that I did not hear them leave.

Lydia: They were here for only a few hours. I let them out and locked the door.

Narrator 2: Lydia changes the subject so that her husband will not question her further about the previous night.

Lydia: We are in need of flour. Since it is a mild day, I thought I would go into the country to Pearson's Mill in Frankford and buy some before the bad winter weather sets in.

William: Why are you going so far?

Lydia: Flour can be purchased only at one of the mills outside the city.

William: How can you get past the British outposts?

Lydia: I will use the pass General Howe gave me when we agreed to let the British use the rooms in our house.

William: I forgot about that. I hope that you are going to take your maid with you.

Lydia: No. I hope to visit our children who are staying with my cousin not far from the mill. The maid will just be in the way.

William: Do you not need her to help you carry the flour?

Lydia: *(stubbornly, but cautious to avoid suspicion)* I can manage it myself.

Narrator 2: William Darragh knows how stubborn and self-reliant his wife is and lets the subject drop. He has his own work to do.

An hour later, Lydia is on her way. She has little time to lose. Whitemarsh is fourteen miles away, and she must walk there. She is a small woman who appears fragile, but she actually has a great deal of stamina. She carries an empty flour sack. She will have it filled on her way back to avoid giving away her real reason for leaving the city.

Act I, Scene 3

Narrator 1: The road between Frankford and Whitemarsh late in the morning of December 3, 1777. After walking half the distance between Philadelphia and the Continental Army's camp, Lydia, now quite cold and weary, realizes that she has to find someone trustworthy to carry her important message to General Washington. She meets an American officer and family friend, Colonel Craig. He is surprised to see the respectable Philadelphia lady walking alone so many miles from her home.

Lydia: *(wearily)* I am so glad to see you, Colonel Craig.

Colonel Craig: *(dismounting from his horse)* Mrs. Darragh, whatever are you doing walking on this road so far from Philadelphia? Don't you realize there is a war going on? You are traveling between two armies.

Lydia: Of course I know there is a war. That is exactly why I am here.

Narrator 2: Lydia, who trusts the colonel, tells him about the secret meeting of General Howe and his officers in her house. She reveals to him the date of the planned surprise attack on General Washington.

Craig: That is very important information. The general has already had four days warning of General Howe's plans, and we have been taking all the proper precautions. But we did not know the actual time of the attack.

Lydia: Will you take this information to General Washington personally? I am afraid that I cannot make the trip and then return home in time without arousing any suspicion among the British or my own family.

Craig: Your family does not know of your venture?

Lydia: No, I did not want them burdened with the information. The fewer people involved in any dangerous matter, the better. They think I have gone to the country to visit our younger children, who are staying with my cousin, and to buy a sack of flour.

Craig: I think that is wise, but I fear for your safety. Before I leave for Whitemarsh with your information, let me bring you to a local farmhouse to rest and eat.

Lydia: That would be kind of you. But first you must promise not to reveal my identity to anyone. If word gets back to

General Howe of my espionage activity, my whole family will be punished.

Craig: I promise. Now get on my horse, and I will bring you to the farmhouse. The sooner you rest and are fed, the quicker you can return to Philadelphia and the fewer questions will be asked.

Narrator 2: After Lydia has something to eat at the farmhouse, she explains her reason for being in the country to the farmer's wife, who also is a loyal American patriot. Lydia wants to make sure that General Washington receives her vital information in case Colonel Craig is stopped by the British on his way to Whitemarsh. She writes her secret in a note and puts it into a small needle and pin case. The farmer's wife offers to bring the case to an American officer who is staying at a local tavern. She is sure he will deliver it to General Washington.

Relieved, Lydia returns to Philadelphia, stopping to see her children and picking up a twenty-five-pound bag of flour. The success of her journey gives her the strength to complete her tasks.

General Washington receives the warning in time to prepare for the assault. The next day, a furious General Howe discovers that the Americans have been warned. He recalls his army back to Philadelphia.

Because the surprise attack was discussed at the Darraghs' house, Lydia is summoned to British headquarters a few days later. The same British officer who was at the secret meeting questions her. Luckily, he remembers how difficult it was to awaken her that night. Lydia is released. Her secret is safe. Her son and his fellow soldiers are spared from what might have been a disastrous battle by Lydia's brave and dauntless actions.

Betty Zane: Horse Thief and Heroine

Characters

Betty Zane — a young lady from a Philadelphia family of loyal American patriots

Colonel Ebenezer Zane — Betty's brother and a patriot who lives in the small settlement of Fort Henry, Virginia

Simon Girty — the British commander of soldiers and Indians

Mr. Adams — an American settler whose family has sought safety in Fort Henry

Lookout — a soldier on duty in Fort Henry

Introduction

Narrator 1: Legend tells us that Betty Zane first proved her bravery and loyalty to the cause of the American patriots while she was attending school and staying with her aunt in Philadelphia. One night, forty British soldiers came to Betty's house demanding food. The servants provided the food as quickly as they could. Meanwhile, Betty was hiding in her second-floor bedroom nervously waiting for the hated enemy to leave. While hiding, she remembered her father's comment that General George Washington badly needed horses for his troops. It occurred to her that there were forty horses currently tethered right outside.

Betty decided that this was a great opportunity to help the Continental Army. She carefully sneaked downstairs and out the front door without being seen by the British soldiers. The careless soldiers had left their horses unguarded. She tied the reins of

each horse to the pommel on the saddle of the preceding horse. Then she led them all off in a chainlike line and delivered them to General Washington's army several miles away.

The British never knew who took their horses, but they held the Zane family under suspicion after that incident. After her aunt died, Betty joined her brother, Colonel Ebenezer Zane, at the small settlement of Fort Henry in an area that was then part of Virginia, where the Wheeling Creek flows into the Ohio River. It was here that Betty performed her most courageous and famous act.

Act I, Scene 1

Narrator 1: Fort Henry, the morning of September 11, 1782. Betty is staying with her brother and his family in a small cabin not far from the fort. All the settlers in the area are now crowded into the stockade that

they built earlier for protection against the Indians. Fort Henry is surrounded by about one hundred fifty British soldiers and two hundred Indians under the command of Simon Girty. The American settlers prepare to defend themselves. Although their numbers are small, about twenty men and forty women and children, they are determined not to surrender. Colonel Ebenezer Zane gives orders in a firm voice.

Colonel Ebenezer Zane: Everyone seems to be here. Bolt the gate, for we may be attacked at any minute. Load your guns and be careful with the gunpowder. Our supply is limited, and every shot must count. *(to the women)* Put the food and stores safely away. We do not know how long we will be under siege.

Betty Zane: Brother, what can I do to help?

Colonel Zane: You can organize the women. Those who are not taking care of small children can keep the powder horns filled, load the rifles, and cast new bullets. We also will need bandages for the wounded.

Betty: I will tear up strips of cloth and have them ready.

Narrator 2: A lookout on the wall yells down to the colonel.

Lookout: A man on horseback carrying a flag of truce is approaching the fort.

Colonel Zane: I will climb on the barricade to see for myself.

Narrator 2: Colonel Zane joins the lookout and shouts down at the horseman riding up to the wall.

Colonel Zane: Who are you?

Simon Girty: *(yelling back in a rough voice)* I am Simon Girty.

Colonel Zane: You notorious scoundrel! What do you want?

Girty: I have three hundred fifty men under my command circling your little fortress. Surrender or be massacred!

Colonel Zane: Never! We are expecting reinforcements at any time. Take your men and leave us in peace.

Girty: No reinforcements will be able to help you.

Narrator 2: Simon Girty rides off angrily, and Colonel Zane climbs back down into the middle of the enclosure below.

Betty: Are we really going to get reinforcements?

Colonel Zane: Only if some come by chance. No one knows of our predicament, and it would be impossible for a messenger to get through that circle of Redcoats and Indians surrounding us. I was hoping to discourage Simon Girty. But I am afraid it did not work. The old rascal is too shrewd to be fooled. Let us get ready now, for this will surely be a long siege.

Narrator 2: Betty leaves to help the women.

Colonel Zane: *(turning to his men)* Since we do not have much gunpowder, every one of your shots has to meet its target. Aim carefully. Our numbers are small, but we can defend our lives and homes if we act wisely and keep up a strong appearance. If our enemies see that we intend to persevere, they might be discouraged and give up. That is our only hope.

Narrator 2: Soon the British and Indians commence their attack. The men, placed strategically along the walls, pick off the attackers one by one without letting up or showing any sign of weakness. The women work bravely beside them, cleaning, cooling, and loading rifles.

Act I, Scene 2

Narrator 1: Fort Henry, the afternoon of September 12, 1782. Although the British and Indians retreat at noon to rest before they begin their attack again, they continue to watch the fort closely. Colonel Zane calls a meeting of all adults in the conclave, except for the few women who are watching the small children. There is tension in the air because everyone is aware that they will soon run out of gunpowder.

Colonel Zane: *(sadly)* We cannot go on much longer. There is only enough gunpowder left for a few shots. We face almost certain defeat.

Betty: There must be a supply of gunpowder somewhere close by.

Colonel Zane: I left a keg hidden in our cabin. We rushed to the fort so fast when we got the warning that the British and the Indians were about to attack us that I did not think to bring it.

Betty: Could someone make a dash for

the cabin and retrieve the keg?

Mr. Adams: The cabin is more than sixty yards away. The British or the Indians will shoot anyone who sets foot outside these walls, never mind anyone who runs to the cabin.

Betty: Why not wait until the cover of darkness? Someone would have a better chance at night.

Colonel Zane: We cannot wait until then. They are sure to attack us once more before sunset, and we will run out of gunpowder by nightfall.

Adams: Then our only chance is to retrieve the gunpowder from your cabin.

Colonel Zane: I am afraid you are right. Do we have a volunteer?

Narrator 2: Several men raise their hands.

Colonel Zane: Only one man should go. We do not have enough men as it is, and we need as many as possible to protect the women and children for as long as we can.

Betty: *(stepping forward)* We cannot afford to lose any man. Why not let me go? I can run fast, and I know your cabin well. I could find the keg and be on my way back in a flash.

Colonel Zane: I cannot let you go. You would be shot as soon as you left the fort.

Betty: The Indians will be so surprised to see a woman that they will not shoot for a while, maybe even long enough for me to get to the cabin. Then your men can cover me with their sharpshooting as I run back to the fort with the keg. What other choice do we have? If we do not get some more gunpowder soon, we are all going to be massacred anyway.

Adams: She has a good point, Colonel.

Colonel Zane: I have to admit that you are right. We might as well not waste any more time. Are you ready to go now, Betty?

> # The Indians and the British do not know what to make of a woman dashing across the field.

Betty: *(without hesitation)* Yes, brother.

Colonel Zane: Then I will tell you where the powder keg is hidden. When you enter the cabin, turn to your right. Do you know where the blanket chest is in the corner?

Betty: *(impatiently)* Yes.

Colonel Zane: The keg is hidden in a hole in the floor under the chest. Please be careful.

Betty: *(anxious to be on her way)* I will, brother.

Narrator 2: The fort's gate opens, and Betty slips out and moves swiftly toward the cabin. The Indians and the British are taken by surprise and do not know what to make of a woman dashing across the field. Only when they realize what her destination is do they open fire. Betty makes it to the cabin, enters, pushes aside the chest, opens the trap door, and lifts out the keg. She then pulls up her long skirt and wraps it around the keg, enabling her to carry it more easily as well as to run faster. Without a minute to lose, she flies out the door and runs back to the fort, dodging bullets and arrows as she goes. Her brother opens the gate for her. Betty enters, exhausted but safe.

The keg is quickly opened, and the gunpowder is distributed among the men. They used up the little gunpowder they had left covering Betty's return. Now with plenty of powder, the men continue to pick off the enemy. Betty never stops to rest. She goes back to helping load and clean rifles and fill powder horns.

Simon Girty leaves the next morning when he realizes that he has been outwitted and that the settlers are not going to quit. Fort Henry is saved, and the last frontier battle of the American Revolution is won because of the bravery of a daring young heroine.

Resource Activities

True or False?

Sybil Ludington

1. Colonel Henry Ludington planned to keep the family's yearling in case of a British attack. The horse would be good if escape was necessary.
2. Abigail Ludington strongly objected to Sybil's ride.
3. Sybil Ludington practiced riding the yearling daily just in case she might be needed by the militiamen.
4. Sybil completed her ride without any major incident.

Lydia Darragh

5. Lydia Darragh, her husband, and her two sons were Colonial spies.
6. Lydia objected to the British using her house as a meeting place because she did not want the younger children so close to the enemy.
7. Lydia told her husband to send someone to find her if she did not return from Whitemarsh by the next day.

Betty Zane

8. The British blamed the Zane family for the loss of forty of their horses.
9. Betty Zane was the only person at Fort Henry who volunteered to fetch more gunpowder.
10. Betty's run for the extra gunpowder saved Fort Henry.

Do You Remember?

Sybil Ludington

1. Why were so few militiamen guarding the storehouses at Danbury, Connecticut?

2. Why did Sybil Ludington ride to the farms and sound the alarm instead of Colonel Ludington?
3. Why did someone have to ride that night? Why did Colonel Ludington have to leave the next morning?
4. Why did Sybil hide when she heard other riders approaching?

Lydia Darragh

5. What secret method had Lydia Darragh often used to send messages to General George Washington?
6. Why were the British so trusting of Lydia?
7. Why did Lydia relay her information about General William Howe's secret meeting to two people?

Betty Zane

8. How was Betty Zane able to lead forty horses to General George Washington by herself?
9. How did Betty and the other women help at Fort Henry?
10. **What was Betty's reasoning for being selected as the volunteer?**

What Do You Think?

Sybil Ludington

1. What could have been some of Colonel Henry Ludington's reasons for not letting the exhausted courier try to alert other farms?
2. Why did some people refuse to put the lights on in their farmhouses when they heard Sybil Ludington's cry?
3. Why was ammunition and gunpowder so important to the Colonials?
4. When Sybil returned home, she saw hundreds of men preparing to march against the

British. What does this tell you about the Dutchess Seventh Militia?

Lydia Darragh

5. What advantages were there to Lydia Darragh's having an older son in the Continental Army and her younger children staying with relatives outside of Philadelphia?
6. Was Lydia's decision not to tell her family of her true mission wise?
7. Why did Lydia not want her maid to accompany her?

Betty Zane

8. Why were there so many women and children in Fort Henry?
9. Why did Colonel Ebenezer Zane relent and expose his sister Betty to such danger?

10. What made Simon Girty end the siege?

From the Historical Perspective

Sybil Ludington

1. What was the biggest difference between the British Army and the Continental Army? How did it affect the performance of the colonists?

Lydia Darragh

2. Why did British officers feel they had the right to enter the Darragh household and use it as their own?

Betty Zane

3. What were the main advantages that the soldiers of the Continental Army and the patriotic colonists had over the British?

Further Activities

Sybil Ludington

1. Research and retrace Paul Revere's ride. Compare and contrast its purpose, length, duration, ground covered, and effectiveness with Sybil Ludington's ride.

Lydia Darragh

2. Who were the Quakers? What was the content of their religious beliefs? How did they help in the Revolutionary War? Do

Quakers exist today? Are they still pacifists?

Betty Zane

3. Research the position taken by the Indians along the frontier during the Revolutionary War. Did the Indians, either as a group or by tribe, side with the British, the colonists, or neither? Research the factors that influenced the military decisions made by the Indians during this period.

THE FOREIGNERS AT VALLEY FORGE

Historical Overview

On July 4, 1776, the great bell in the State House of Philadelphia rang to announce the Declaration of Independence. Soon newspapers everywhere proclaimed the event: The thirteen colonies had become the United States of America, a new nation subject not to England's laws but to its own. Patriotism and the revolutionary spirit ran high, but the war was still to be fought. The Continental Congress authorized an army made up of recruits from each colony. Congress also appointed George Washington as commander in chief because of his proven leadership in the French and Indian War. Every colony also had its militia, local units composed of volunteers who were ready to fight on a moment's notice.

Congress knew, however, that patriotism and courage were not enough to defeat England. Ammunition, weapons, and artillery also were needed. Yet even these were not as important as additional manpower to fight the British and money to buy supplies and pay the soldiers. Congress tried to resolve part of this problem by issuing U.S. currency. International merchants, however, feared that the United States was not strong enough financially or politically and hesitated to accept the money. Consequently, the money had little value

and was considered worthless by many. Soldiers who needed money to support themselves and their families had to be staunch, loyal patriots to serve in the army. This lack of financial support caused many soldiers to desert and others to refuse to enlist.

Congress quickly realized that to succeed, the new nation had to win the support of foreign allies. France and Holland were the principal targets of U.S. diplomacy. France frequently faced England on the battlefield. In the 1760s, France lost the French and Indian War to England. Its people and government still sought revenge for this defeat. Holland's merchants were wealthy and were always seeking to expand their trading ventures.

Late in 1776, Congress met with Benjamin Franklin, a statesman who was well respected throughout the Colonies for his outspoken views in defense of the Revolution. Franklin was asked to travel to France and seek aid and funds from King Louis XVI. Franklin undertook the mission, but Louis XVI and his noblemen refused to commit themselves to the cause. They could not conceive of a fledgling nation defeating so great a power as England.

Not all Europeans were as noncommittal as Louis XVI. Europe was at peace, no wars were under way, and there were many trained soldiers whose services the colonists would greatly appreciate. Many cheered the patriots and left their homelands to assist and enlist in the Continental Army. Several officers performed such distinguished service that their names became linked with the Revolution and its eventual outcome.

From France came the Marquis de Lafayette, a young nobleman who fought bravely and worked tirelessly to encourage his country's entry into the war. From Poland came Thaddeus Kosciusko, a military engineer who helped design the defense works at Bemis Heights in New York and the fortifications at West Point, and Casimir Pulaski, an officer who helped drill the patriots, especially the cavalry units. From Germany came Baron Johann de Kalb, a secret agent of France who had originally been sent to check out the situation in the Colonies, and Baron Friedrich Wilhelm von Steuben, who trained the soldiers at Valley Forge and organized them into a disciplined fighting unit. From Spain came Bernardo de Galvez, the governor of the Spanish province of Louisiana, who opened the port of New Orleans to American ships, captured British ships dedicated to smuggling, and supplied funding and necessities such as clothing and gunpowder to the American forces.

On occasion, difficulties occurred when ranking positions were awarded to foreign officers. General Washington and others, however, tried their best to act as fairly as possible, always aware that their decisions could affect the outcome of the war.

There were other difficulties. Congress did not always appropriate enough funds, or, when it did, the funds failed to arrive. Congress also spent considerable time discussing how the war should be fought and what was necessary to govern efficiently. Battles and skirmishes, however, did not wait for its approval.

The year 1777 was full of defeats for the Americans. The British defeated General Washington and wounded Lafayette at the Battle of Brandywine, just outside of Philadelphia. The British took Philadelphia,

in effect splitting the Colonies into two camps—those in New England and those in the South. The British Navy also controlled the seas, outmaneuvering whatever ships Congress was able to man and outfit. The Americans, however, did gain one very important victory—the defeat of General Bourgoyne's troops at Saratoga, New York, on October 17, 1777. This victory is now considered the turning point of the war. When news reached France about Saratoga, Louis XVI changed his position about the Americans winning the war. Accordingly, he pledged French support. But because of the time it took for news to travel in 1777, Washington did not learn of Louis XVI's decision to send troops until the spring of 1778.

The winter of 1777 was a difficult one for the Americans. The war seemed endless. Patriotic spirit ran high, but the continued hardships and lack of necessities made many people rethink their positions. Victories such as the one at Saratoga raised morale and rekindled hopes of success. But it was not until foreign involvement began that wretched winter of 1777–78 that the Americans ultimately strengthened their position and prepared themselves for victory.

George Washington and the Foreigners at Valley Forge

Characters

George Washington — the commander in chief of the Continental Army

Marquis de Lafayette — a young Frenchman who came to the United States to help the Revolutionary cause

Baron Friedrich Wilhelm von Steuben — a veteran army officer from Prussia and an expert on military discipline

John Laurens — an interpreter and a lieutenant colonel in the Continental Army

---

Introduction

Narrator 1: General George Washington brought his army of eleven thousand men to Valley Forge, Pennsylvania, on December 19, 1777. They stayed there until June 19, 1778. These six months were marked by incredible hardships of cold weather and snow, starvation, deadly diseases, and inadequate clothing and shelter. They also symbolized the courage and perseverance of the Continental Army. At the end of these months of persistence and dedication, a well-organized, united, and competent army emerged.

Many foreigners decided to join America and its Revolution against tyranny because of the determination of the men at Valley Forge. General Washington was partial to foreign officers, a preference that often caused resentment among his American officers. His decision to use foreigners, however, proved sensible and wise in the end. The quiet, serious resolution of the Americans and the experience of the Euro-peans combined to bring about a victory for freedom and the birth of a new nation.

Act I, Scene 1

Narrator 2: It is the end of December 1777. The Continental Army is settled in Valley Forge for the winter. A military camp of about one thousand log huts and earthworks for defense has been built quickly. General Washington moved out of the army tent he was using as headquarters on Christmas Day and is now renting a house from Mrs. Deborah Hewes.

The general is ready to tackle some of the many problems that have arisen since the move from Whitemarsh. One problem is how to use the many foreign officers who have volunteered to help the Americans. Washington deals with this matter with his usual good sense and patience. His attitude of diplomatic good will is obvious, especially toward the young Marquis de Lafayette.

The twenty-year-old French marquis be-

came enamored of America, its people, and their fight for freedom when he arrived earlier that year from Europe. Lafayette is from a wealthy, well-connected family high in the ranks of French nobility, and his friendship with the new, struggling nation is certainly welcome. General Washington understandably takes to this engaging Frenchman and readily accepts his offer of service.

The two men meet in one of the parlors in the general's headquarters. Lafayette enters the room and embraces General Washington. They sit down in two armchairs in front of a fire that hardly takes the chill out of the air. Their animated conversation fills the room, and the warmth of their friendship is obvious.

George Washington: I am so glad to see you. Much has happened since our last meeting. I apologize for this cold, damp room. Even the fire does not provide much heat. But it is warmer than the tent I was in last week. My office will eventually be in the rear of the house. I cannot move into it until they complete a log cabin in the back that will become the dining room.

Marquis de Lafayette: I am happy to be here. I have missed our talks. You have been like a father to me since I came to your country.

Washington: Have you heard from your young wife in France?

Lafayette: Yes, she is well but misses me.

Washington: That is understandable. When do you plan to see her again?

Lafayette: I hope to return to France in a year to be reunited with her. We hope to have a son whom I will name George Washington Lafayette as a tribute to you.

Washington: I am honored. My respect for you as a gentleman, friend, and companion is returned.

Lafayette: I also plan to recruit military help from my government for your country when I return to my homeland. I will be the liaison officer between your government and the French, especially between you and Rochambeau, the commander of the French expeditionary force.

Washington: I have great confidence in you, and I will be pleased to have you represent me. I value your connections. Your family holds high diplomatic, military, and court positions at Versailles that will be of help to us.

Lafayette: My wife also is well connected. She is the daughter of the duke of Noailles.

Washington: We are indeed fortunate to have you with us. How is the leg wound you received in September at the Battle of Brandywine?

Lafayette: I was in the hospital for several weeks, but it is healed now. It bothers me only when the weather is cold and damp, like now.

Washington: You have already acquired an impressive military record. After your bravery at Brandywine, you distinguished yourself on November 25 at the Battle of Gloucester with your skill and courage. That is why I recommended that Congress give you the command of a division.

Lafayette: I truly appreciate your recommendation.

Washington: You deserve it.

Lafayette: I will serve without pay, as you do. The prospect of winning glory in America will be enough reward for me.

Washington: You will have the chance to win much glory for yourself and for our young nation. We have some tough months ahead of us. The British are an impressive foe and will not give up easily.

Lafayette: I have waited to serve under you since Congress appointed me a major general on July 31, 1777. I mistakenly assumed that the command of a division would immediately accompany this rank. Later I realized that this was really only an honorary appointment. I was disappointed because one of my reasons for coming to America was to serve under you. My dream has finally come true.

Washington: Both Congress and I were hesitant because you were only nineteen years old. We were not aware of your value to us at the time. I began to take notice of your ability and importance when I heard from Benjamin Franklin, who is representing our nation in Paris. He said to take special care of you. After our first meeting with some members of Congress at the City Tavern in Philadelphia, I decided to have you join our military campaign.

Lafayette: That first meeting is still clear in my mind. I was wearing my brand-new major general's scarf. I remember being impressed by the majesty of your presence. You were easy to distinguish from the officers and other people who were around you. It was clear that I was in the company of simple and unassuming nobility. My impatience to join your forces must have been obvious.

Washington: I remember your hazel eyes sparkled with such enthusiasm. You seemed eager to impress me, but you were shy. Your English was broken, though I must compliment you on the progress you have made in a few months. It's probably because of your tireless determination. My overall impression was that you were worthy of respect and attention. It was then that I had the notion to invite you to regard me as both a friend and a father.

Lafayette: I accepted your kind offer willingly and gratefully, for my own father died when I was only two years old. No other man has replaced him in my life.

Washington: You are now a special part of my military family as well.

Lafayette: I hope you will not forget the other French officers who came with me to America. Could they not also be given commissions?

Washington: No, that would be unfair to my American officers who have already proven their worth and loyalty on the battlefield and in this cold, poorly equipped camp.

Lafayette: Nevertheless, I will continue to convince my countrymen of the importance of your cause and struggle for independence. Their chance to join your military family may come at a later date. Meanwhile, I am tied to your destiny, and I shall be faithful to it and support it by my sword and by all other means in my power.

Narrator 2: General Washington is visibly moved by the devotion of the young marquis. The two men stand, shake hands, and then go their separate ways, for there is much to be done at Valley Forge.

Act II, Scene 1

Narrator 1: It is February 1778 at Valley Forge. Prussian general Baron Friedrich

> *"You will have the chance to win much glory for yourself and for our young nation."*

Wilhelm von Steuben has just traveled from Boston to York, Pennsylvania, and then on to Valley Forge by sleigh with his military secretary. He plans to volunteer his services and sword to General George Washington and the Continental Army.

Washington is very pleased to have von Steuben join him. He rides to meet the baron and accompany him the last few miles to Valley Forge. When the two men arrive at the camp, they are greeted by an officer and a twenty-five-man honor guard at the baron's new quarters. Von Steuben inspects his honor guard with General Washington. Aide-de-camp John Laurens acts as an interpreter.

Baron Friedrich Wilhelm von Steuben: I am very honored by this guard that has greeted me so impressively upon my arrival at your camp, but I must decline it. I wish to be considered simply as a volunteer.

Washington: *(answering the baron politely)* The entire Continental Army would be pleased to stand guard for such a volunteer.

von Steuben: *(visibly touched)* You are too kind. After my long, cold journey, I am grateful for such a warm welcome.

Washington: You must be tired. Rest for a day or two, and then we will talk at my headquarters. Today your name will be given as watchword. Tomorrow my army will be mustered, and I would be pleased if you would accompany me to review it.

von Steuben: I will be honored to join you. I am anxious to discuss your army's circumstance and what I can do to help.

Washington: I look forward to our meeting. I have awaited your visit with special interest ever since I received your letter from Portsmouth on January 8 along with a note of introduction from Benjamin Franklin.

Narrator 2: The two men part. The baron retires for a much-needed rest, and Washington returns to his headquarters to continue dealing with the never-ending problems of a war-ravaged army.

Act II, Scene 2

Narrator 1: General Washington's office at the rear of his headquarters two days later. Washington and von Steuben meet, accompanied by interpreter John Laurens.

Washington: We are honored to have you with us.

von Steuben: The honor is mine, General Washington. If the greatest general of Europe or even Prince Ferdinand of Brunswick had been in my place, he would not have been greeted with more honor.

Washington: I trust you rested well. Unfortunately, your quarters are probably not what you were used to in Europe.

von Steuben: I am rested, thank you. I have stayed in worse places. Fortunately, I can sleep under just about any conditions. What has shocked me, though, is the condition of your army. Your soldiers looked more like a herd of cows than trained, organized troops when I watched them marching yesterday.

Narrator 2: Washington is shocked at the baron's bluntness but impressed by his honesty and directness.

Washington: It embarrasses me to agree with you, but what you say is true. My men are loyal and determined to fight for freedom, but they are, for the most part, poorly trained, undisciplined amateur soldiers. Our supplies are very low. My soldiers have little food and clothing, and many do not even have a decent pair of shoes. In addition, the men have been weakened by an epidemic of colds and smallpox. Morale is low.

von Steuben: Morale is low in my staff, too. In fact, my cook was so disgusted with your camp that he has left to return to France.

Washington: We have executed deserters and spies as examples. But we must do more to discipline our army, or we will not be very effective against the British.

von Steuben: I offer you my services. I am not known as an old war-horse of a soldier for nothing.

Washington: I have plans for you. We certainly do need your experience. But first, tell me about yourself.

von Steuben: I have a long background in the military. My father was an officer in the German Army. I have served as a Prussian regular army officer and an aide to Frederick the Great, the German emperor. I also have been the grand marshal of Prince Hohenzollern Heckingen.

Washington: When did you become interested in the American cause?

von Steuben: My military career ended several years ago, and since then I have traveled extensively. While visiting Paris, I met your countryman Benjamin Franklin. It was because of my conversation with him that I became attracted to your young nation and its quest for freedom. When I expressed interest, some American agents asked me to come here and train your Continental Army. Apparently they were attracted by my reputation as a disciplinarian and my skill in training precision marching to infantrymen. I was then offered a commission as a general in your army, and here

> *"I know of no European army that would have stayed together and endured such poor health and lack of food."*

I am, at your service.

Washington: My army certainly needs proper training. That is one of the problems of a young nation; we do not have experience in many important areas.

von Steuben: The ability to drill is vital when fighting the British, for their ranks march into battle as precisely as if they were on a parade ground marching for the king.

Washington: I had not thought of that. You make a good point. I need a replacement for an officer I have not been pleased with, a General Conway. Since you are a volunteer as well as a foreigner, will you become our acting inspector general and new drillmaster? I do not want to offend my American generals and give you a special commission as major general. They are touchy on the subject of foreign generals in the American Army. I am sure, however, that they will like and respect you due to your rank and experience.

von Steuben: I understand, and I appreciate your honesty. I will be honored to train your men. They might be cold and tattered, but in the short time I have been here, I recognize in them a solid determination that is superior to any I have ever seen. I know of no European army that would have stayed together and endured such poor health and lack of food, clothing, and shelter.

Washington: I am proud of my men and have confidence in them. But they need direction. We are fortunate to have the advantage of a lull in the war to begin training the troops. You just have to tolerate the complaints and the weather.

von Steuben: I am used to the cold winters of Germany. The complaints will end when your men realize that they are being trained into a tough, orderly fighting force.

Washington: I will arrange for you to visit several regiments. Take notice of the problems, deficiencies, and faults that you see so that you can advise me as to the best methods to solve them.

von Steuben: I have just one request. Captain Duponceau, a member of my staff who accompanies me as an interpreter, is not familiar with American customs, nor does he have much knowledge of military affairs. Your young aide here (*pointing to John Laurens, who has been interpreting for the two men*) seems very intelligent and useful. Could I have him to assist Captain Duponceau? If I am to train your officers and their soldiers, I must be able to communicate with them.

Washington: Of course! It is a sensible request. (*turning to John Laurens*) John, you are assigned to General von Steuben for as long as he needs you.

John Laurens: Yes, sir. It will be my pleasure.

Washington: *(turning back to von Steuben and rising)* We both have much to do. Please report back to me of your progress. Let me know if I can be of help in any way. I also will ask Major General Nathanael Greene, one of the best soldiers in the Continental Army, to assist you.

von Steuben: Thank you, General. I am anxious to begin my lessons in basic discipline at once.

Narrator 2: The two men shake hands and go their separate ways.

Act II, Scene 3

Narrator 1: A month later in the dining room of General Washington's headquarters. Over dinner, von Steuben, Washington, and Captain Duponceau discuss the baron's progress with the American troops.

Washington: I have followed your progress closely and have heard positive reports from my officers. They all think highly of your abilities. Tell me what you have accomplished.

von Steuben: I began by picking a company of men and drilling them so they could serve as a model for the other companies. I taught them the basics, such as how to stand at attention, how to turn right face and left face, and simple marching rules. I soon became aggravated. But this seemed to amuse the men, and they responded to my oaths, even though I had to find somone to translate them into English. My German and French oaths were not at all effective.

Washington: *(laughing)* I would not think so.

von Steuben: We drilled every day from sunrise to sunset on the muddy fields. When I was satisfied with the training of these men, I sent them back to their units with a drillmaster to teach their fellow soldiers by example. Then I trained another company and repeated the process.

Washington: That is a very practical method of teaching.

von Steuben: It is the only way to accomplish this huge task. Soon all the soldiers of Valley Forge will be trained by this model method, and they by example will transmit the drilling procedure to the entire Continental Army.

Washington: Our country is already in debt to you. Your influence will even be felt in the future.

von Steuben: I hope so.

Washington: I am interested in hearing your opinion of our American men.

von Steuben: I am fascinated by your independent and lively Americans. In my country, when an officer tells a soldier to do something, he does it without asking any questions. Here in America, you must first explain why you ought to do something before a soldier will do it.

Washington: *(laughing again)* You have learned of our free spirit. I am glad. Our freedom to question is one of the rights for which we are fighting.

von Steuben: It also is important that General Greene is providing the army with better equipment.

Washington: Yes, that has been a necessity. I am pleased with your progress. If nothing else, you have given my army the will to fight on.

von Steuben: That is true. When a soldier grows in skills, he also grows in pride. You will soon have a new army.

Washington: Our nation is grateful to you.

Narrator 2: Baron von Steuben continues drilling his model companies, and before long the entire army is trained. Washington and his officers consider this progress a miracle. New recruits begin to arrive with an organized staff ready to train them.

Every man who survives that terrible winter at Valley Forge feels that the experience has made him a better soldier. They are now confident that they can defeat the British. This confidence and a trained military organization are Baron von Steuben's contributions to a new nation's war for independence. Even today, the old Prussian war-horse's influence is still present whenever a drillmaster trains new recruits.

Resource Activities

True or False?

1. George Washington's military camp at Valley Forge was ready before he arrived with his troops in December 1777.
2. George Washington first met the Marquis de Lafayette at Valley Forge.
3. Lafayette told Washington that he was planning to return to France to solicit help for the young United States from his government.
4. Washington promised Lafayette that he would commission the other French officers who had come to join the Continental Army in the fight against Great Britain.
5. Washington had heard of Baron Friedrich Wilhelm von Steuben's military skills and had sent for him to come to Valley Forge.
6. Von Steuben had a long history as a military man and officer in Europe. He had served as an aide to the German emperor Frederick the Great.
7. Every morning, von Steuben drilled all the men at Valley Forge.
8. After he began the drill program, von Steuben did not stay long at Valley Forge. The conditions were too depressing.

Do You Remember?

1. What command was the Marquis de Lafayette given in July 1777 when Congress appointed him major general?
2. How did Lafayette plan to express his admiration for George Washington?
3. What type of pay did Lafayette expect for his service to the Continental Army?
4. Did Lafayette fight in any battles prior to being given the command of a division?
5. Who wrote Baron Friedrich Wilhelm von Steuben a letter of introduction for General Washington?
6. What did von Steuben think of the soldiers in the Continental Army when he first reviewed them?
7. Why did von Steuben feel so strongly about training the American troops?
8. What fascinated von Steuben most about the American troops?

What Do You Think?

1. Why was the Marquis de Lafayette's social position in France so important to George Washington and the American troops?
2. Why did Lafayette have such a genuine admiration for Washington, though he had known him only briefly?
3. Should Washington have commissioned more foreigners as officers if their expertise was greater than that of the American soldiers?
4. What did Washington like about Lafayette?
5. Many historians believe that without Baron Friedrich Wilhelm von Steuben's training at Valley Forge, the Americans' chances of victory would have been minimal. Why?
6. Von Steuben barked orders to the army at Valley Forge and was relentless in his training, yet the soldiers followed his orders. Why?
7. Why did the soldiers in the Continental Army question von Steuben's commands?
8. Besides being a strict drillmaster, what other personality traits do you think von Steuben possessed?

From the Historical Perspective

1. George Washington and Congress both agreed that the United States needed allies in the war against England. Why did they consider French involvement in the American Revolution so important?

2. Baron Friedrich Wilhelm von Steuben was shocked at the lack of clothing and rations among the Continental Army. Why were clothing and food supplies so low?

Further Activities

1. The Marquis de Lafayette contributed greatly to the success of the American Revolution. Research how the United States repaid his service. Why did Lafayette return to the United States in 1824, and what type of welcome did he receive?

2. Baron Friedrich Wilhelm von Steuben and many other foreigners volunteered their services to the Continental Army. Research the Hessians, Europeans who sold their services to the British and fought as mercenaries in the Revolutionary War.

Discuss the different backgrounds of von Steuben and the Hessians.

3. Foreigners played a major role in the Revolutionary War. Yet foreign powers were reluctant to ally themselves with the newly formed United States. France and Spain eventually joined forces with the Americans. Research how Spain contributed to the Revolutionary cause, the reasons for its hesitation to commit itself, and the debt due the Spanish governor of Louisiana, Bernardo de Galvez.

THE VICTORIOUS MARCH TO VINCENNES

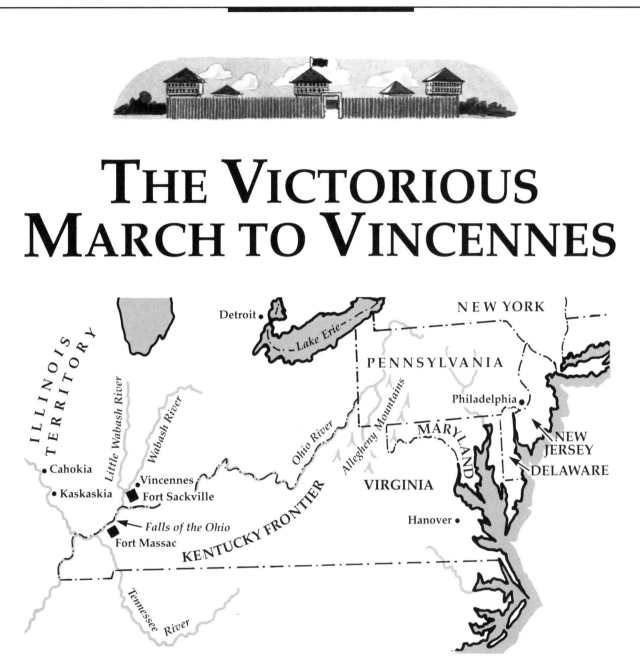

Historical Overview

While the soldiers of the Continental Army and the patriots fighting in the various militia throughout the thirteen colonies fought most of the battles of the Revolution on the East Coast, battles and skirmishes did rage in the little explored and sparsely settled lands west of the Appalachian Mountains.

France had once claimed ownership of the lands reaching from the Appalachian Mountains across the Mississippi River to the Rocky Mountains. After losing the French and Indian War to England in 1763, France gave the lands east of the Mississippi to England and the lands west of the Mississippi and Florida to Spain. That same year, the British issued the Proclamation Line of 1763, which prohibited colonists from settling on any lands west of the Appalachian Mountains. This law was passed to help traders in these territories and to prevent trouble between settlers and the Indians, to whom these lands had belonged for centuries.

Not everyone observed the Proclamation Line of 1763. Many traders and settlers, including those of French origin, refused to leave. As a result, the loyalties of the inhabitants of these western lands varied greatly during the Revolutionary War.

The Indians, on whose lands many of the battles were fought, found themselves in an especially difficult situation. Some Indian chiefs and leaders argued that it was best not to choose sides or even fight in the revolution. Others argued that the Indians should fight and defeat the white men who had stolen their lands. All this added to the conflict, especially along the frontier.

The new American government did not have the resources or the troops to wage war against the British on all fronts. Instead, the leaders concentrated on defending or recapturing cities and ports in the East.

There were, however, several Americans who devoted themselves to defending and protecting the interior and the frontier. Francis Marion, known as the Swamp Fox, waged guerrilla warfare in and around the swamps and forests of South Carolina. While Marion and his courageous rebels did not fight any major battles, their tactics and tireless harassment wore down the British. As a result, their contributions, while often unmentioned, actually brought the Revolutionary War to a much faster close.

Another fighter in the West was George Rogers Clark. He loved the open frontier and knew the customs and habits of the Indians who inhabited this area. When the Revolutionary War broke out, Clark was determined to prevent British troops from infiltrating and gaining control of the western outposts. His friends Daniel Boone and Simon Kenton sought the same goal: freedom to roam and settle Kentucky and the lands west of the Appalachian Mountains with no interference or regulations from England.

Clark decided this could be done only by defeating the British at their headquarters at Fort Detroit. With permission and encouragement from Patrick Henry, governor of Virginia, Clark began his march northward. After he captured Fort Sackville at Vincennes, he renamed it Fort Patrick Henry in honor of the famed statesman who had believed in him.

Unfortunately, Clark did not continue on to Detroit as he had planned. He and his men, who were tired, hungry, and ragged, chose to wait for the reinforcements that had been promised. But the reinforcements did not arrive. Many historians believe that Clark could have defeated the British and captured Fort Detroit if he had continued on from Vincennes. The lack of men and supplies prevented him from doing so, despite the fact that he went into debt to reequip his men and buy food.

During the Revolution, many people in the East thought it a waste of precious ammunition, money, and supplies to outfit troops fighting along the western frontier when the Continental Army was having such a difficult time defending the East Coast.

After the Revolution, many easterners packed their belongings and headed west to find a better life. These new frontier people owed much to the courage and steadfastness of soldiers such as George Rogers Clark who defended the settlers and defeated the British against all odds.

George Rogers Clark and the March to Vincennes

Characters

George Rogers Clark — a colonel in the Continental Army and a frontiersman from Virginia

Patrick Henry — the governor of Virginia

Lieutenant William Linn — an officer in Clark's army

John Saunders — a frontier guide used by Clark

Simon Kenton — a friend and officer in Clark's army

Father Pierre Gibault — a French Roman Catholic priest

Captain Joseph Bowman — an officer in Clark's army

Captain John Rogers — an officer in Clark's army

Willie Chalmers — a fourteen-year-old drummer boy in Clark's army

Introduction

Narrator 1: The 1779 march of Colonel George Rogers Clark and his American soldiers against the British at the former French settlement of Vincennes is said by many to be the most adventurous and the boldest expedition of the American Revolution in the West.

Clark was an influential and forceful man from Kentucky. He often warned about the danger that the thousands of Indians in the area presented to the settlements. He repeatedly reported to American officials that the British were bribing these Indians to come to their side. One Englishman, Lieutenant Colonel Henry Hamilton of Detroit, was especially guilty of exciting many tribes against the settlers. The Indians in general were angry and suspicious of all white people because they were rapidly taking over their lands. They did not need to be convinced to go to war against the Americans or the British. Most Americans who tried to settle anywhere west of the Ohio River were killed or driven back to the East. Every group of colonists that came down the Ohio River by boat was attacked by the British or the Indians.

Clark's plan to eliminate the British threat in Kentucky and the lands west of the Allegheny Mountains included the capture of their headquarters in Detroit. But first, he argued, they must capture the smaller settlements of Cahokia, Kaskaskia, and Vincennes in southern Illinois. He realized that this could be achieved only by traveling a great distance through wilderness and by confronting many dangers along the way. Clark was prepared to endure any hardships necessary to defend Kentucky against the British and to free the lands in the West from their control.

Act I, Scene 1

Narrator 2: It is a cold December day in 1777 at the home of Patrick Henry, governor of Virginia. George Rogers Clark has traveled seven hundred miles to meet with the governor, who is recovering from an illness at his estate in Hanover. Clark seeks Henry's support for a plan to protect Kentucky and the lands in the West from the British and the Indians.

Henry, who has been called the "Firebrand of the Revolution," has listened with amusement and admiration to Clark describe the dangers of the Kentucky frontier. He is impressed by his sincerity and enthusiasm.

George Rogers Clark: How are you feeling?

Patrick Henry: Better now that I have rested here in the quiet surroundings of my estate.

Clark: I apologize for bothering you during your convalescence, but I must speak with you. Kentucky is in danger.

Henry: *(grinning)* This is not the first time I have heard you speak with some urgency about your frontier land. It was a year ago that I helped you convince the executive council to give your Kentuckians five hundred pounds of gunpowder.

Clark: And that was not without a fight. They were willing to give me the powder, but they would not pay for its transportation.

Henry: I remember.

Clark: I reminded your councilmen that Kentucky protected Virginia's borders from the Indians.

Henry: I seem to remember your using a stronger argument.

Clark: Yes, I told them that if a country is not worth protecting, it is not worth claiming. I also hinted that some other country, specifically England, might think it worth some attention. That statement got me my ammunition and its transportation to Kentucky.

Henry: Good for you! How safe are our frontiers now?

Clark: Sir, that is the reason I have come to you. Thousands of Cherokee, Delaware, Miami, Mingo, Ottawa, Wyandot, and Indians of other tribes are a threat to our settlements. Our greatest danger, though, is the British.

Henry: Why is that?

Clark: The Redcoats are bribing the tribes with woolen blankets, liquor, weapons, and gunpowder.

Henry: Where did you get this information?

Clark: I sent some of my men to scout the area west of the Alleghenies. They brought back word that Lieutenant Colonel Henry Hamilton has been stirring up many tribes against our settlers. It has been rumored that he pays Indians to bring him American scalps. He has been nicknamed "Hair-Buyer" Hamilton.

Henry: I have heard that rumor. Unfortunately, not much can be said about this practice because American settlers are also said to be paying Indians for British scalps.

Clark: The Indians are irate because their lands are being taken over by white people. It is not difficult to convince them to go on the warpath.

Henry: Unfortunately, from what I have heard, they trust the English more than they trust us.

Clark: That is true.

Henry: How do you suggest we deal with this Indian threat and the Redcoats?

Clark: American soldiers must capture Detroit, where the British have their headquarters.

"Yes, I told them that if a country is not worth protecting, it is not worth claiming."

Henry: That is easier said than done.

Narrator 2: The Kentuckian lays out on a table a map that covers the area from Wisconsin and Illinois to Pennsylvania and Virginia.

Clark: We should first march into southern Illinois and capture Cahokia, Kaskaskia, and Vincennes. *(pointing to the map)* From these small settlements nearest to Kentucky, we could reach and overcome the Indians. Then we would have advance bases against the British in Detroit.

Henry: When you go to war within an enemy's country, you have to know what is going on there. You must know how many British soldiers there are as well as where the loyalty of the French militia lies and how the French inhabitants feel about the British.

Clark: That is true. We have plenty of agents and spies who will keep us informed of the enemy's strengths, weaknesses, and movements. I also think that we can rely on some help from the French. They do not like the English, and I am sure we can persuade them to come over to our side.

Henry: Do not forget that the enemy has spies everywhere in the Ohio Valley. Your plans and movements must be kept from them, for the element of surprise is essential to your success.

Narrator 2: Henry studies Clark's map and considers his plan. He looks up from the map and speaks with a gleam in his eye.

Henry: This is a very risky venture. Will you be leading this march?

Clark: *(indignantly)* Of course!

Henry: You have my approval, but only under certain conditions. I will tell the leaders of my executive council, but no one else should know of your plans. This will be an expedition supported by Virginia, not one approved by the Continental Congress. There is no time for that. You are right that Kentucky is Virginia's protection against the Indians as well as the British, who now have a strong foothold in the West. How many men do you think you will need?

Clark: I would like about five hundred men, but secrecy will make it difficult to find recruits.

Henry: If word gets out about how dangerous this mission is, you will have trouble getting volunteers.

Clark: I had not thought of that. I must begin at once. Thank you for your support. You will not regret approving my plan.

Henry: We are indeed fortunate to have such an eager and enthusiastic leader on our side. Good luck.

Clark: Thank you.

Narrator 2: The two men shake hands. Clark leaves to begin looking for recruits for his march.

Act II, Scene 1

Narrator 1: It is late June 1778 deep in the heart of enemy country. George Rogers Clark has managed to recruit only 275 men instead of the 500 he wanted. Rumors of the dangers of his venture have leaked out, and most men, though anxious to protect the frontier and their homes from Indian and British attacks, do not want to risk their lives in unknown lands.

The shortage of recruits does not stop Clark. He puts his men on bateaux, large flatboats with galleys of oars, on the river near the Falls of the Ohio River, travels through the rapids, and eventually lands at Fort Massac about ten miles from the mouth of the Tennessee River. These brave men then head through thick forests to capture the fortified settlements of Kaskaskia on the Kaskaskia River and Cahokia on the Mississippi River.

Clark's camp is at the edge of a forest. He and his men, after hiding their bateaux in a little narrow inlet, have been traveling northwest toward Kaskaskia for three days. They have marched about fifty miles in single file following the marks of an old French military road and leaving as little evidence of their passing as possible. While Clark and his men are resting, they discuss the journey and their next move.

Clark: Although marching through woods, like all wilderness travel, is very tiring, I prefer it to traveling on open prairie. At least the woods conceal you.

Lieutenant William Linn: We have been lucky. We have seen neither Indians nor British soldiers.

Clark: And I do not think that we have been observed either. We also have been fortunate that our food has held out for four days.

Linn: Not having wagons or pack animals is a problem. Our men can carry only so much on their backs. We are lucky that the blackberries, dewberries, and raspberries are ripe. It has been difficult to keep the men moving when we pass patches loaded with berries. The men also would like some venison to have with their fruit. Could some of them go hunting?

Clark: No! We cannot risk shooting a rifle unnecessarily. We might give away our position. Here on the frontier, everyone knows the sound of each other's rifle, and a strange shot would cause alarm.

Narrator 2: Clark calls over to their guide, John Saunders, who is pacing nervously nearby.

Clark: John, why are you so nervous?

> *"If word gets out about how dangerous this mission is, you will have trouble getting volunteers."*

John Saunders: *(eyes downcast and embarrassed)* I have lost my way.

Clark: *(eyes blazing with anger)* You have lost your way! I thought you had been to Kaskaskia recently.

Saunders: I was. I simply lost my bearings.

Clark: *(very irritated)* Why did you know your way through dense woods but lose it when we entered open plains?

Saunders: *(ashamed)* I do not know.

Clark: From my own experience, I know how easy it is to get lost, but we are in a dangerous situation and cannot afford any mistakes. *(sharply)* If you cannot find the trail by nightfall, then prepare to die!

Narrator 2: Shaken, Saunders leaves to search for the trail, knowing Clark is serious. Clark turns to the officers around him.

Clark: We must not let word of this get out to the men. You know how fast bad news travels in a camp. We cannot have our troops put into confusion. While we wait for our guide to return, let me

tell you my plans. We are probably outnumbered by the militia at Kaskaskia, and they, I am sure, can get help from the nearby Indian tribes. Our only chance is to make an immediate surprise attack tonight. Then they will not know how few men we have, and we might be able to bluff them.

Simon Kenton: What if Saunders cannot guide us to Kaskaskia?

Clark: He has to. My threat seemed to be enough to make him find his way. When we capture the settlement, our men must be on their best behavior. If our soldiers are destructive, act rough, or get out of line, the French in the area will turn against us and side with the British. We need their help. I would like as many French recruits as pos-

sible for our march to Cahokia and then to Vincennes. Word will have spread by then of our arrival, and the British will be prepared for us.

Kenton: Saunders has returned!

Narrator 2: The guide, looking relieved, walks over to Clark and his officers.

Clark: Did you find your way?

Saunders: Yes, Colonel. The road that leads to Kaskaskia is not far from our camp.

Clark: Good! *(turning to his officers)* Now go to your soldiers and tell them to rest. We march in a few hours at dusk when we will not be seen. Also remember to warn them about their behavior when we arrive at Kaskaskia. This is crucial to our ultimate success against the British. We need the French as allies. We want them to respect and even fear us a little but not hate us. We also must guard all the roads leading out of Kaskaskia, for we do not want the British to find out about our presence in the area.

Narrator 2: After resting, Clark and his men travel several miles until they come to a farmhouse. They find some boats there and use them to cross the Kaskaskia River to the fort on the opposite bank that guards the settlement. The Americans enter the fort without being noticed. Everyone is asleep, including the sentry. Clark and Kenton awaken the lieutenant governor, who is stunned.

The inhabitants of the town become alarmed when they realize what has happened. They are quickly calmed down, sent back to their houses, and told by the French-speaking Americans to stay there.

Clark and his men take Kaskaskia without firing a shot or aggravating the French. The inhabitants' initial fear of the Americans is soon replaced by good will and friendship.

Act II, Scene 2

Narrator 1: A month later in the commander's headquarters at the fort at Kaskaskia. Clark is meeting here with Father Pierre Gibault, the local Roman Catholic priest, who is very influential in the area, dislikes the British, and has become fond of the young American colonel. The priest is relieved to find out that Clark, a Protestant, has no intention of forcing his religion on anyone.

Clark: Welcome back, Father. I trust you have some news for me.

Father Pierre Gibault: Yes, Colonel Clark, I do. But first I cannot help but notice how much different you look now than when I met you here last month.

Clark: *(chuckling)* Yes, I remember. My officers and I had left most of our clothing at the river crossing, and we wore blankets to cover ourselves.

Father Gibault: Your tanned skin was all scratched and cut by bushes and briers.

Clark: We must have looked like savages.

Father Gibault: Worse, I think.

Clark: What news do you have from Vincennes? Does an American or British flag fly over the fort?

Father Gibault: I am pleased to report that it is the American flag.

Clark: *(delighted)* Now we should have an easier time of capturing Detroit. But we must not act hastily. Our men need more training before we can attack the Redcoats at their headquarters. And we need more supplies. At least we will not have to waste time fighting them at Vincennes. We can use the town and neighboring Fort Sackville from which to move on Detroit.

Father Gibault: Have you captured Cahokia yet?

> *"You have done well to conquer so peacefully. All wars should be conducted in this way."*

Clark: Yes, and again without firing a shot. I was advised by the citizens of Kaskaskia that the French villagers of Cahokia could be persuaded to surrender peacefully. So I sent one of my men, Joseph Bowman, and several leading citizens of Kaskaskia to Cahokia, where no one had any idea that we had captured this settlement. The people of Cahokia were not about to fight or argue with fellow Frenchmen on the side of the hated British. They surrendered and swore an oath of allegiance to our young American nation.

Father Gibault: Were there any Indians there?

Clark: Yes, but they left immediately when they realized what had happened.

Father Gibault: It is good to have Cahokia on your side.

Clark: Yes. Now we have more recruits to choose from for our journey to Vincennes and the ultimate goal of Detroit.

Father Gibault: You have done well to conquer so peacefully. All wars should be conducted in this way.

Clark: Father, tell me more about the situation in Vincennes.

Narrator 2: The priest reports as many details as he can recall for about half an hour.

Clark: I think I will send Captain Leonard Helm and a companion on ahead to take command of the militia at Vincennes. I will have them join me when we move on to capture Detroit from the British. *(shaking hands with the priest)* Thank you for your services, Father. You have helped our young nation greatly.

Narrator 2: Clark's good fortune is not to last. The British commander at Detroit, Lieutenant Colonel Henry Hamilton, is not happy that the American flag flies over Vincennes and Fort Sackville. He takes a force

of 162 soldiers and about 70 Indians and marches to Vincennes. Along the way, he recruits more Indians and arrives at Fort Sackville with a good-sized force. The militia there, now under the command of Captain Helm, is forced to surrender when it sees the large number of Redcoats and Indians surrounding the fort. The American flag is replaced by the British Union Jack.

Colonel Hamilton does not want word to get out that the fort has returned to British hands, so he places guards on all the trails and roads leading out of the settlement. He hopes to trap Clark, but he makes one mistake. He allows a Spanish merchant, Francis Vigo, to leave. The Spaniard has promised to go to St. Louis, but as soon as he arrives there, he leaves to warn Clark.

Act III, Scene 1

Narrator 1: It is February 1779. George Rogers Clark, in his headquarters at the fort in Kaskaskia, receives word from Francis Vigo that the British have taken Fort Sackville at Vincennes. He is now completing plans for his march to recapture the settlement for the Americans.

Vincennes, the largest French settlement in the Illinois area, must be taken, for only then can Clark and his troops go on to Detroit and free the area from British rule. Capturing Vincennes also is a necessary step toward making these lands available for settlement by Americans and safe from Indian attack.

Clark is concerned that Colonel Hamilton will receive reinforcements, especially from the Indians, if the Americans do not act quickly. Thus, a surprise attack is crucial to the success of his campaign. Even with recruits from Kaskaskia and Cahokia, Clark has only about one hundred seventy men. He is relying on the fact that Hamilton will never expect the Americans to march miles through drowned prairies and flooded swamps in the middle of the winter to get to Fort Sackville. Indeed, Hamilton does underestimate the determined colonel from Kentucky and his courageous followers.

Clark is arranging for a boat to transport some soldiers, weapons, and supplies. He discusses his plans with Father Gibault and his officers.

Clark: Thank you, Father, for helping enlist Frenchmen for our march to Vincennes. We need every man we can get.

Father Gibault: I am happy to do my part to free this land from the British.

Clark: I would like you to bless my men before we depart on our journey. My Protestant soldiers will only vaguely understand what you are doing, but it will be appreciated by the many French Catholics who make up our little army.

Father Gibault: That is a nice gesture. I will be glad to give a short lecture on the purpose and then give everyone absolution.

Clark: That will be fine. *(turning to his officers)* I have bought a bateau. It is to be named the *Willing* in honor of the courageous captain whose boat came down the Ohio River before us more than a year ago. Simon, I want you to organize a group of men to convert the boat into a small warship.

Simon Kenton: Yes, sir. How much time do we have?

Clark: I want it finished in two days.

Kenton: How shall I arm it?

Clark: With two four-pound cannon, four large swivel cannon, and one nine-pound cannon.

Kenton: I will start at once.

Narrator 2: Kenton leaves to gather a work force to begin transforming the bateau into a warship. Clark turns to Captain John Rogers, a strong, handsome officer who has the reputation of being kind and careful with his men.

Clark: John, I am placing the *Willing* under your command. I know that you are an officer of mounted soldiers, but you must now double as a naval commander. If anyone can get it through to the Wabash River, you can.

Captain John Rogers: Yes, sir. I will be honored.

Clark: You will need forty men to row the boat. Take the recruits from Cahokia.

Rogers: When do we leave?

Clark: In three days. You will sail down the Kaskaskia River to the Mississippi, then ascend the Ohio River until you come to the Wabash. Make the best time you can.

Rogers: Where should we stop?

Clark: About thirty miles south of Vincennes. Wait there until you receive further orders from me.

Rogers: Yes, sir. Do you have any other orders?

Clark: Yes. You are not to allow any hostile boats to pass you down the river. I do not want to take any chances of allowing Hamilton to escape. If he should try, you must block his way. You also must keep your presence on the river concealed from the British and their Indian allies. If you are discovered, fight. I do not want Hamilton to suspect that we are on our way to Vincennes. I suggest that you use scouts along the riverbanks to warn you of any vessel coming your way. I also think that you should station riflemen around the *Willing* to guard it when you are anchored on the Wabash waiting for me.

Rogers: I will do as you say.

Clark: Your mission is crucial to our success. You will be carrying our artillery, ammunition, and stores. We also will need

> *Clark is arranging for a boat to transport some soldiers, weapons, and supplies.*

your boat to transport us across the last few miles of cold, flooded waters to Vincennes.

Rogers: I will not disappoint you, sir.

Clark: I am sure you will not. That is why I chose you to take this command. I will be at the dock to see you off on February 4. The rest of our troops and I will depart the following day by land.

Narrator 2: Rogers leaves to help Simon Kenton and his men prepare the *Willing*. At two o'clock in the afternoon on February 4, the *Willing* leaves Kaskaskia. The transformed boat is admired by everyone. The British have no vessel in the area to match this warship. For once, the Americans have naval supremacy, at least on the Wabash River.

Act III, Scene 2

Narrator 1: A small island of dry land in the middle of the flooded prairie between Kaskaskia and Vincennes. It is February 12, 1779, and Clark and his men, exhausted, hungry, cold, and wet, have been marching in the rain and through waist-high water for a week. They have stopped for the night and are feasting on buffalo and venison that the soldiers shot during the day's journey. Clark and his officers eat their meal around a blazing fire and discuss the past weary week as well as the future.

Simon Kenton: I have never seen so much rain.

Captain Joseph Bowman: It has become such an ordinary occurrence that you do not even notice it after a while.

Kenton: That is true, but it is difficult to tolerate without waterproof boots, shoes, or clothing.

Lieutenant William Linn: It is exhaust-

ing wading through such deep water. You have to lift your legs up high, and your feet get stuck in the mud underneath as well.

Kenton: Sometimes the water has been up to the men's armpits or their chins. They have had to carry their muskets above their heads to keep them from rusting and to keep their gunpowder dry. That effort is exhausting.

Clark: I know morale is low. No one has been comfortable during the day or at night. It is difficult to sleep in wet clothes on damp ground. But we must keep our spirits up. If we do not take Vincennes and "Hair-Buyer" Hamilton by surprise, our meager army will not succeed. He will never expect us to march under these conditions.

Kenton: No one would.

Linn: Why are so many areas flooded? In the woods and hills of Kentucky and Virginia, the water either soaks into the ground or runs off.

Bowman: The packed earth of the flat Illinois prairie keeps the water from sinking into the ground as it does in forests with porous organic floors. And there are no hills for the water to run off. Thus the water from rain and snow rests on top of the earth for a long time before it eventually drains off or evaporates.

Linn: At least tonight we have dry land to sleep on and hot food to eat. Colonel, your idea of having each company take turns inviting the other companies to dinner has worked.

Clark: I am pleased with the results. I gave the host company extra horses to carry in the meat. It was impossible to try to stop our men, who are mostly hunters, from shooting the buffalo and deer that are so plentiful around here. Each company has the excitement of preparing for the night's

meal and entertainment. It also gives the others something to look forward to at the end of a long, exhausting day.

Linn: Buffalo meat is not that tasty this time of year, but the tongue and hump are good.

Kenton: I have enjoyed the entertainment each company has provided after each meal. They are like lively Indian war dances.

Bowman: (*laughing*) Even you, Colonel, blackened your face and ran about whooping like an Indian.

Clark: I have to show my enthusiasm so our men will keep their hopes up. We all must do our best to raise the morale of our soldiers. That is why I encourage singing during the day. It helps get the men's minds off all the hardships they are encountering.

Linn: Singing songs as we are marching is a good idea. I especially like your solos.

Clark: (*joking*) I knew that hidden talent of mine would come in handy someday.

Bowman: Our little fourteen-year-old drummer boy from Cahokia, Willie Chalmers, has been a great morale booster.

I must admit that I doubted your wisdom in bringing him along at first.

Clark: I had my own doubts as well, but his enthusiasm and perseverance shame the most weary men. Nothing fazes him.

Linn: His comical songs and infectious laughter have cheered us all, even during the most dismal times.

Clark: He pleaded with me to take him with us, and I am glad I did. The poor little tyke has no one. His family was slaughtered by hostile Indians before we arrived. He was the only survivor. He was starved and almost dead when we found him. Simon and I wrapped him in furs and nursed him back to life.

Linn: We are his family now. We need him, and he needs us.

Kenton: That is for certain.

Clark: (*yawning*) It is time to retire. We must leave early. We have miles ahead of us, and we have to take advantage of this high, dry ground to get a good night's sleep. Who knows when we will see dry land again.

Narrator 2: The men all rise to find a comfortable spot for the night.

Act III, Scene 3

Narrator 1: The Wabash River and Little Wabash River on February 23, 1779. Clark and his men are on the last leg of their march. But their greatest obstacle now confronts them—two flooded, raging rivers. Three miles of dry land usually separate the Little Wabash and Wabash rivers. But all the excess rain has caused the rivers to flow together above where they join, making a very wide expanse of water three feet deep and much deeper in the channels.

The soldiers build a raft to ferry the supplies across to a platform that has been erected on the other side. The horses wade to the river channels and then swim to the platform, where they are reloaded with the supplies. Then it is the men's turn to cross the water.

Although dry, hilly land can be seen five miles to the east, the worn-out army's plight appears nearly hopeless. But their fiery leader and dauntless drummer boy plan to plunge ahead. They all heard the British morning and evening guns go off at Fort Sackville the day before, and they know Vincennes is not far away.

Clark: Simon, go with some men in a canoe to the far banks of the Wabash River to see if our Cahokian friends and Captain Rogers have arrived yet. We need the recruits and supplies badly because we are only about nine miles from Vincennes. Once we cross this water, we must head for Fort Sackville as soon as we can and take the British by surprise.

Kenton: Yes, Colonel. *(leaves)*

Clark: *(turning to the other officers)* We have sent the horses and what supplies we have left to the platform we erected on the opposite bank. Now we must join them by wading across.

Narrator 2: Clark plunges into the water, and his soldiers follow. Some men cling to floating logs, and the weaker men are transported on a raft. The rest wade through the freezing water holding their muskets above their heads.

Clark: *(turning to the drummer boy)* Are you with me, Willie?

Willie Chalmers: Yes, sir. I will drum up some enthusiasm.

Narrator 2: Willie has been riding on the shoulders of a large soldier because the water is too deep for him. He jumps off the soldier, sits on his drum, and begins to float across the water, paddling with his feet. He then begins to sing comical songs. The sight of this brave boy bobbing on a drum and singing makes the discouraged men laugh, and they all reach dry land by nightfall.

The next day, a canoe paddled by Indian squaws and laden with buffalo meat, corn, and tallow comes up the river. The soldiers capture it and eat the supplies. Clark and his army rest a short while before setting out for Fort Sackville. Simon Kenton returns from looking for the *Willing*.

Clark: Simon, did you have any luck?

Kenton: No, Colonel. There was no sign of the *Willing*. We searched for several miles along the Wabash River.

Clark: We cannot wait any longer for it. We must set out for Vincennes. It is just over the hill, and the men are anxious to capture the fort. We do not have a minute to lose.

Narrator 2: That night, Clark and his men surround Fort Sackville. By the next day, the surprised and furious Colonel Hamilton surrenders. The march to Vincennes is a success.

> *The sight of this brave boy bobbing on a drum and singing makes the discouraged men laugh.*

Resource Activities

True or False?

1. In general, the Indians in the West trusted the British more than they did the Americans.

2. Governor Patrick Henry did not feel that George Rogers Clark would have any problems recruiting volunteers for his planned attack on the British headquarters in Detroit and the major outposts leading to Detroit.

3. Before Patrick Henry approved Clark's military plan, he wanted to get the approval of the Continental Congress.

4. John Saunders, Clark's guide, lost his way on the march to Vincennes.

5. Clark carefully planned his conquest of Kaskaskia and trusted that his men would behave themselves once the settlement was captured.

6. Clark captured Vincennes without firing a shot. At Cahokia, however, the inhabitants resisted, and Clark's men were forced to use their guns.

7. When Henry Hamilton, the British colonel, learned that Clark had raised the American flag above Fort Sackville at Vincennes, he led his own troops to recapture Vincennes and take Clark prisoner.

8. Clark planned to have a boat carry his artillery and ammunition to a spot thirty miles south of Vincennes. This would save his men the extra burden of carrying such heavy loads.

9. Clark brought drummer boy Willie Chalmers along because he knew that the boy's spirit and liveliness would cheer his troops.

10. Clark was anxious about his ammunition and supplies arriving on time by boat. He was relieved when he learned they were there to greet him on the Wabash River.

Do You Remember?

1. What argument did George Rogers Clark use to convince the executive council of Virginia that it should support his efforts on the frontier?

2. What was the nickname given to British lieutenant colonel Henry Hamilton and why?

3. How many men did Clark feel he needed to attack and set up advance bases at Cahokia, Kaskaskia, and Vincennes? How many did he actually recruit?

4. Why did Clark forbid his men to hunt on their march to Kaskaskia?

5. Food supplies were a constant problem for Clark on the march to Kaskaskia. What helped ease his men's hunger?

6. When Clark learned that Vincennes was flying an American flag, why did he not prepare to march against Detroit?

7. What did Father Pierre Gibault like best about Clark's victories?

8. How did Clark learn that Colonel Hamilton had taken control of Fort Sackville at Vincennes?

9. Why was surprise essential to Clark's capture of Vincennes?

10. Why was the area on the way to Vincennes flooded?

What Do You Think?

1. Why was Patrick Henry willing to support Clark?

2. Why did Clark not want his men to learn about John Saunders's losing his bearings on the way to Vincennes?

3. Was Clark's argument that if land is not worth protecting, it is not worth claiming sound?

4. Why was Clark's ultimatum to Saunders

("find the trail or die") so strong?

5. Why was Father Pierre Gibault's support an important factor in Clark's success?

6. Why did Captain Leonard Helm surrender Fort Sackville at Vincennes to Colonel Henry Hamilton?

7. Why did the Spanish informer Francis Vigo go to St. Louis first and not directly to Clark?

8. Why did Captain John Rogers have to be so careful as he piloted the *Willing* upriver?

9. Why did Clark allow his men to hunt buffalo on the march to Vincennes?

10. Why was Clark's participation in the evening entertainment important?

From the Historical Perspective

1. Colonel Henry Hamilton allowed only a Spanish merchant, Francis Vigo, to leave Fort Sackville. What lands belonged to Spain, and what trading were the Spanish doing in the New World?

2. Why was it necessary for the colonists to protect the frontier during the Revolution?

3. History often focuses only on the Revolutionary battles fought along the eastern coast of the thirteen colonies. Why have the battles and skirmishes fought in the western lands been neglected or omitted?

Further Activities

1. Research the French presence west of the Allegheny Mountains at the time of the American Revolution. Research the lands along the Mississippi River discovered by French explorers such as Sieur de La Salle and the plan to settle thousands of French in the Ohio Valley in 1748.

2. Research the states that were carved out of the territory in which George Rogers Clark fought and marched. Mark them out on a map.

3. Find out more about George Rogers Clark. What did he do before organizing troops to march on Detroit? What happened to him after the march to Vincennes?

REVOLUTION AT SEA

Historical Overview

In the 1760s and 1770s, many people throughout the thirteen colonies disagreed with the new laws being passed by the English Parliament. Some colonists refused to obey them. Others tried to convince Parliament to change its policies.

For years, England allowed the colonists in the New World to govern themselves and set many of their own policies. It was a long way across the Atlantic Ocean, and England had other concerns besides America. Various battles and wars, often with France, required most of England's troops and funds. The English Parliament did pass laws concerning the colonists but often did not enforce them strictly. The colonists certainly did not complain. This policy made the colonists quite self-sufficient and used to governing themselves.

The French and Indian War from 1757 to 1763 changed this situation. When England defeated the French, its prize included all the lands west of the Appalachian Mountains to the Mississippi River, except for New Orleans and Florida. But England also was in debt because the war had been so costly. To pay the debt, England decided to tax the colonists, since they had benefited most from the war.

This time England not only passed new tax laws but also chose to enforce them. As the colonists took sides for and against England, few thought the discussion would

end in another war. The colonists were especially unprepared. They were not soldiers; they had no military training. All military ammunition and artillery in the Colonies belonged by right to the British.

Yet war did come. American volunteers banded together and prepared to defend the cause of freedom. British storehouses of ammunition were raided and forts captured. The new Continental Army encountered many difficulties, especially a lack of supplies and worthless pay. (Continental money was considered to have no value by many merchants.)

The British, on the other hand, were already prepared for war. Many British soldiers had fought in battles in Europe. Money was no problem, and many British even used gold as currency. Supplies also were sufficient, since England commanded the seas and could transport food and other necessities easily. In fact, control of the seas was England's great advantage. Its ships could blockade Colonial ports and prevent other countries' ships from entering with needed supplies.

The colonists did not have time to build a fleet, nor did Congress have the money to fund a fleet. Instead, the colonists used merchant ships that crisscrossed the Atlantic transporting goods. Congress gave merchant ships permission to make war on any enemy ships they encountered. Many Colonial merchant ships became privateers that harassed the British fleet.

When France entered the Revolution, it

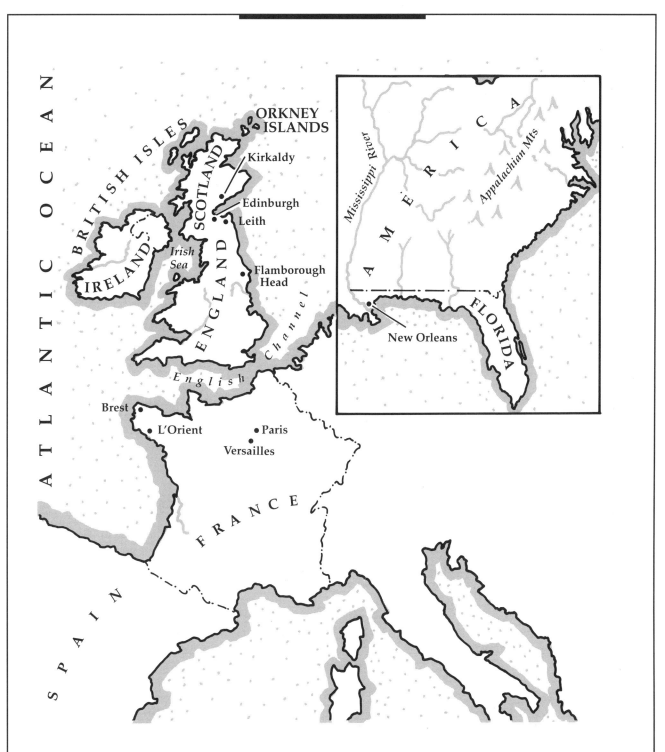

supplied the Americans not only with troops and money but also with warships. While the French ships proved effective, the privateers also were effective.

The most daring of American sea captains was John Paul Jones, a Scotsman who had emigrated to the United States.

He was the first and only seaman daring enough to cross the Atlantic and attack the British at home. Under his command, his crew sank many English merchant ships and did much damage to British trade and commerce.

The *Bon Homme Richard* and John Paul Jones

Characters

John Paul Jones — a daring American naval captain

Benjamin Franklin — a famous writer, inventor, and statesman and the American ambassador to France

Lieutenant Colonel de Chamillard — an officer under Jones

Lieutenant Richard Dale — an officer under Jones

Master Trent — the sail master of the *Bon Homme Richard*

Captain Richard Pearson — the captain of the British ship *Serapis*

Captain of the *Vengeance*

Captain of the *Pallas*

Introduction

Narrator 1: All of Europe had nothing but praise for John Paul Jones. No enemy ship had ever cleared the English Channel and the Irish Sea of British merchant vessels before the time of this daring American captain. Nor had any British ship ever been set ablaze in an English port by an enemy vessel. Jones was the first person in seven centuries to lead an invading force across the green lands of Britain.

Captain Jones had captured the English naval ship the *Drake* in British waters with his much slower ship, the *Ranger*. When he arrived in the French port of Brest with his prize, he found that France had acknowledged the independence of the American Colonies and had openly sided with the young nation against Britain. Warships with French crews and officers were attacking British vessels, and French troops were being sent to America. Furthermore, Benjamin Franklin, the American ambassador to France, was a favorite of Paris society.

This alliance with France was the opportunity for which Jones had been waiting. Perhaps he would now be given command of the fast, sturdy ship he thought he deserved instead of the slow, weak vessels he had been commanding.

The Continental Congress had not made use of Jones's capable services because the American Navy was in disarray. The war with Britain was costly, and Congress was short of money. Now Jones could turn to Louis XVI, the king of France, for a proper warship and for money to equip it with a crew and sufficient supplies.

Act I, Scene 1

Narrator 2: It is June 1779. John Paul Jones has sent the *Ranger* back to America

while he remains in France with the hope of being provided with a bigger, faster, and stronger warship from the French king. Urged by Benjamin Franklin, Captain Jones makes several appeals to the minister of the marine as well as other authorities in the French government. Many ships are put into commission, but the commands are given to French naval officers. Disappointed, Jones meets with Franklin in his Paris hotel room and asks for help in obtaining the command of a proper ship.

Benjamin Franklin: I heard that you were offered the command of an English prize that was recently captured and brought into the harbor of Brest.

John Paul Jones: Yes, sir. I went to examine the vessel and found the craft very slow. I declined the commission.

Franklin: Why are you so particular? I would think that you would be happy to have been offered a ship after waiting for so many months.

Jones: I do not want to have any connection with a ship that is not well made or is too small.

Franklin: Exactly what do you want?

Jones: I would like a frigate that sails fast and is large enough to carry at least twenty-eight guns, not less than twelve-pounders, on one deck.

Franklin: That is a big order.

Jones: I have big plans. I intend to do the British great harm. I would rather be shot on shore than go to sea in a weak vessel. After I have won so many victories, it is an insult to be stranded on land and to be inactive. I have already wasted much valuable time, and I do not want to waste any effort on a small ship.

Franklin: Why have you not gone to King Louis XVI personally?

Jones: I hoped that the efforts of my friends at the court of the king at Versailles would be sufficient.

Franklin: I think that it is time to ask the king yourself. You have nothing to lose.

Narrator 2: Jones, pacing around the room nervously, picks up an old copy of *Poor Richard's Almanac*, a publication of wise proverbs and witty sayings written by Franklin, and leafs through it. He stops on one page and laughs.

Jones: Here is the answer to my problem: "If you wish to have any business done faithfully and expeditiously, go and do it yourself. Otherwise, send someone."

Franklin: *(chuckling)* That is exactly the advice I gave you.

Jones: You are right. I will go to Versailles today!

Narrator 2: Jones closes the book, putting it on a table, grabs his coat, and heads for the door. He reaches Versailles by nightfall. Because of his reputation, he is easily granted an interview with the king. Louis XVI is impressed with the American captain's outspoken, determined nature, and Jones is given the command of the *Duc de Duras*, an old nine-hundred-ton French merchant ship that has been in the East Indian trade for years. Although worm-eaten and in need of repair, the vessel

> *Louis XVI is impressed with the American captain's outspoken, determined nature.*

mounts forty guns and has much potential. Jones is pleased and immediately begins plans to recondition the ship and make it ready for warfare.

Act I, Scene 2

Narrator 1: The harbor of L'Orient in France five days later. Jones examines his new ship and makes plans with Master Trent, his sail master, and Lieutenant Richard Dale, an American naval officer and friend, for turning the *Duc de Duras* into a frigate and for recruiting a crew. Jones stands on the dock looking at his ship.

Jones: It is a fairly well-modeled ship. It has the promise of being good at sea.

Lieutentant Richard Dale: The ship has one of the high-pitched poops that were so common decades ago. It gives the stern the appearance of high towers.

Master Trent: You can tell that originally it was a single-deck ship and that the cannon were mounted on one gun deck except for those few mounted on the quarter-deck and forecastle.

Dale: It looks as though there are twelve-pounders mounted on the gun deck.

Jones: Yes, there are twenty-eight of them. There also are eight long nine-pound cannon on the quarter-deck and forecastle.

Trent: Sir, are you going to add any?

Jones: Yes. I am going to add six long eighteen-pounders, which will be mounted in the gunroom below. That will give the ship a total of forty-two guns. I just wish they were not so old and worn-out. I hope they do not blow up when we use them.

Dale: What about a crew?

Jones: I am going to have to rely on

whatever crew members I can get. Most of my seventeen officers, especially those stationed on the quarter-decks and forward, will be Americans. I am fortunate because there are not many sailors from America in France at this time. Out of my forty-three petty officers, twenty-seven of them will be British deserters.

Dale: That will be taking a risk.

Jones: What choice do I have? At least they are experienced sailors.

Trent: What about the rest of the crew?

Jones: I have signed up 144 sailors—46 Americans, 54 British deserters, and the rest a mixture of Portuguese, Norwegians, Germans, Spaniards, Swedes, Italians, Malays, Scots, and Irishmen. The French government is allowing me to take about 135 marines, some of whom are to be armed with the latest rifled muskets, to keep order among this undisciplined crowd.

Dale: Will any other vessels be sailing with us?

Jones: We will be accompanied by the new powerful thirty-two-gun frigate the *Alliance*, which was built in America. The vessel has an American crew but is commanded by Captain Pierre Landais, a French officer. He is an experienced navy man, but I think that our Continental Congress made a mistake by giving him the command of one of our ships. I do not trust him. I have heard that he is a treacherous man.

Dale: That will not make for a very trustworthy ally.

Jones: Again, what choice do I have?

Dale: What other consorts will be accompanying us?

Jones: We will be joined by three smaller vessels built in France with completely French crews: the *Pallas*, an old merchant-

man recently remodeled with thirty-two guns; the *Cerf*, a dispatch boat with eighteen guns; and the *Vengeance*, a smaller corvette with twelve guns. We must hope that all these French officers will obey my orders when we are in battle. So few of our men will be Americans fighting for their country.

Trent: Sir, do you intend to keep the name *Duc de Duras* for your ship?

Jones: No. I plan to apply to the French government for permission to change its name to the *Bon Homme Richard*, which means the "Poor Richard." This is to show my gratitude to the wise advice that I read in Benjamin Franklin's book, *Poor Richard's Almanac*. It has brought me such good fortune.

Dale: That is a proper tribute to a gentleman who has done so much for our young nation.

Narrator 2: The three men depart, going their separate ways to begin preparations for the conversion of the *Duc de Duras* to the *Bon Homme Richard*.

Act II, Scene 1

Narrator 1: It is summer 1779. More than three months have passed since John Paul Jones received command of the *Bon Homme Richard*. Although he is given the title commander in chief, Jones has trouble enforcing his authority. The Frenchmen in command of the other vessels often disobey his orders, and some of them prove to be poor seamen. The *Alliance* runs into the *Bon Homme Richard*, losing its mizzenmast and tearing away the head and bowsprit of Jones's vessel.

On August 14, 1779, the ships leave the harbor of L'Orient. The crew of the *Bon Homme Richard* has been increased by about

one hundred American seamen who were sent to France from Britain in exchange for some British prisoners. Two French privateers, the *Monsieur* and the *Granville*, join the little squadron, and they all head north up the west coast of Ireland, capturing enemy ships and sending them back to France. Along the way, the *Monsieur* and the *Granville* leave the fleet because of a disagreement. The *Cerf* also ends up retreating back to France after losing its way in fog and then getting caught in a violent gale. Jones has a disagreement with Captain Landais, and the *Alliance* goes on its way independently of the remaining vessels, not to appear again for several days.

Despite these problems, the little fleet continues looking for prizes and sails around the Orkney Islands and to the north of the British Isles before heading south down the east coast of Scotland. The daring American captain even hopes to do some raiding on land, something that has not happened in Britain for hundreds of years. The inhabitants of Scotland and England are terrified of Jones and expect an invasion at any time.

Jones anchors the *Bon Homme Richard* off the Scottish port of Leith, the prosperous seaport of the city of Edinburgh, which is located a few miles inland. It is the night of September 14, 1779. Jones attempts to convince the captains of the *Vengeance* and the *Pallas* to attack the ships in the harbor and hold the town for ransom.

Jones: This is the type of opportunity I have been waiting for. Leith has a harbor full of merchant ships. The people of the town are asleep, and they have no idea we are now at the entrance to their harbor waiting for the moment to attack.

Captain of the *Vengeance*: Are there any armed vessels in the harbor?

Jones: I sent a small boat in to spy. Only one vessel has twenty cannon.

Captain of the *Pallas*: Are there any shore batteries around the port?

Jones: There are none.

Captain of the *Vengeance*: What is your plan to take the town?

Jones: As the first ray of the sun comes over the eastern horizon, our three ships should dash into the harbor, capture some important prisoners, shoot up and burn as many ships as possible, and quickly return to the open sea.

Captain of the *Pallas*: That is a great deal of maneuvering for our three vessels to do in a harbor full of ships.

Captain of the *Vengeance*: The wind will have to be to our advantage.

Jones: Then we will land troops under the command of Lieutenant Colonel de Chamillard. He will hand the mayor of Leith a letter written by me demanding a ransom to keep us from ransacking and destroying his town.

Narrator 2: The two French captains agree to this plan, and Jones sits down to compose the letter. An hour later, he calls the captains back into his cabin and reads them the letter for their approval.

Jones: This is the letter that Lieutenant Colonel de Chamillard will deliver to the mayor in my name: "I do not wish to distress the people of Leith. My only intention is to demand that you contribute

Jones anchors the **Bon Homme Richard** *off Leith, the prosperous seaport of the city of Edinburgh.*

toward the reimbursement that your country owes to the much-harmed citizens of America. Savages would be embarrassed at the cowardly offenses that have characterized British tyranny in our country.

"Leith now lays at our mercy. And if I were not a humane person, I would have burned it to the ground without any warning. But instead, as my strict duty as an officer requires me, I propose that you raise a reasonable ransom to prevent such a scene of destruction and horror. For this reason, I have given my officer, Lieutenant Colonel de Chamillard, the authority to compromise on the terms of an acceptable ransom. You will be allowed one-half hour to accept or reject the terms that he will propose." *(looking up at the two captains)* Do you approve of this letter?

Captain of the *Vengeance*: It is a clever letter and a fair request.

Captain of the *Pallas*: The town cannot but accept it, and there will be little bloodshed or destruction on either side.

Jones: Good. Then let us prepare to enter the harbor. Dawn is not far away.

Narrator 2: Captain Jones then chooses the landing parties, maps out the order of attack, and explains to the other captains the part to be taken by each of the ships' crews. The two French captains quickly return to their vessels after they receive their orders, and the three ships head for Leith as the sun rises over the town.

As they sail into the bay, the ships pass the village of Kirkaldy. It is a Sunday morning, and the people are at church. But when they see the dreaded foreign warship and its companions offshore, they head for the nearby beach. Legend has it that their elderly pastor, surrounded by his parishioners, offered a powerful plea to God to save his people from the invading Americans.

Suddenly the wind changes direction, and a violent gale begins to blow offshore. The three ships cannot make any headway. As the storm increases in intensity, they head back out to sea to avoid being dashed onto the rocky coast by the waves.

Jones, continuing down the coast of Scotland, finds it difficult to accept the failure of his plan. The people of Kirkaldy are convinced that their neighbors in Leith were saved by the personal influence of their pastor with God. They hold him in high esteem for the rest of his life.

Act II, Scene 2

Narrator 1: It is September 23, 1779. Jones and his crew sail off the cliffs of Flamborough Head on the east coast of England. The *Alliance* has rejoined the *Bon Homme Richard*, the *Vengeance*, and the *Pallas*.

Jones has just sighted a convoy of forty-one British merchant ships escorted by two warships, the newly built *Serapis* with forty-four guns and the much smaller *Countess of Scarborough* with twenty-two guns. This is the richest prize the Americans have encountered, and Jones is ready for a battle, especially after the severe disappointment of the week before at Leith. The American captain knows he is on the threshold of his greatest victory. Jones discusses the exciting opportunity before him with his officers on the *Bon Homme Richard*.

Jones: I am delighted that we have come across such a rich prize of British ships.

Lieutenant Colonel de Chamillard: And they are guarded by only two warships.

Jones: I have longed for a real battle since we left France. I have not enjoyed burning helpless merchant ships and terrorizing defenseless towns and villages. This is our chance to meet the British in a fair fight, cannon to cannon, with even odds on both sides.

Dale: But we are a fleet of four ships, sir, to their two warships.

Jones: I will order the *Vengeance* to help us, but the French captain and crew have not been very supportive. As for the *Alliance*, I do not trust Captain Landais. His behavior is so hard to predict, and he is unreliable. One day he is sailing with us, and then he is off on his own for several days.

Chamillard: A light wind is keeping us from coming close enough to fire on the warships.

Jones: Let us hope that the winds will change by evening. *(turning to his officer)* Begin preparations to attack. Call the crew to quarters and signal the *Alliance, Vengeance,* and *Pallas* to form a line of battle as we sail closer to the enemy. *(looking out over the sea)* I feel a change in the wind already. Our sails are filling out, and waves are forming. We should be upon the British ships by nightfall.

Narrator 2: The sea turns gray and the sky darkens as the sun sets over the English coast. Mixed feelings of fear and excitement spread among the crews as they ready their cannon or work at the ropes of their ships.

The crews of the *Bon Homme Richard* and the *Pallas* go cheerfully about their tasks, but, as Captain Jones predicted, the *Alliance* and the *Vengeance* sail off, leaving the other two vessels to attack the enemy alone.

Captain Richard Pearson of the *Serapis* is proud of his recently built ship. It carries twenty eighteen-pound cannon and twenty-four six- and nine-pound guns. When he sights the dreaded American fleet, Captain Pearson immediately orders the merchant ships in his convoy to sail for the safety of an English fort on the nearby coast. He then heads his ship straight for the *Bon Homme Richard* and commands the *Countess of Scarborough* to follow. There is no question in the mind of this English captain that he has to confront the Americans, and he does so with confidence.

At about seven o'clock in the evening, the two big warships sail toward each other. Rows of open portholes lighted by battle lanterns outline the positions of the ships against the dark sky. Officers on both vessels walk up and down the decks encouraging the men.

Jones is on the quarter-deck with his officers, carefully watching the approaching *Serapis* through a night glass. When the sun sets, the wind dies down to a light breeze and the two ships float slowly together. Suddenly the stillness of the night is broken by a loud voice from the British warship.

Captain Richard Pearson: What ship is that?

Jones: *(replying loudly)* What did you say?

Pearson: What ship is that? If you do not answer me immediately, I will open fire into you!

Narrator 2: Captain Jones answers with a broadside of cannon fire into the hull of the *Serapis*. At once the British ship's battery of cannon return fire on the *Bon Homme Richard,* and one of the most famous battles of naval history begins.

During this first discharge, two of the American vessel's largest cannon, old eighteen-pounders, burst on its lower gun deck, hurling large masses of iron in every direc-

At once the British ship's battery of cannon return fire on the **Bon Homme Richard.**

tion. Jones calls down from his position on the quarter-deck.

Jones: What was that explosion?

Dale: Two of the eighteen-pounders exploded, sir!

Jones: Are there many casualties?

Dale: Yes, sir. Most of the men in the gunroom have been killed or wounded by flying pieces of iron or splinters, and several hunks of iron have crashed through to the upper deck, injuring men stationed there. All our eighteen-pounders are now useless. The men refuse to fire the few that are not damaged for fear that they also will blow up because they are so old.

Jones: At first I thought that the gunpowder magazine had blown up. We are lucky that did not happen. We will now have to fight a ship that has a battery of twenty eighteen-pound guns with our remaining twelve-pounders. But we must not give up! Keep firing our remaining cannon into the *Serapis.* I will join the men and cheer them on.

Narrator 1: Jones leaves the quarter-deck and rushes about among his crew, urging them to continue fighting even though they have already suffered great losses. Seeing their captain's enthusiasm, the men regain their confidence, and the battle rages on. The two big warships try to maneuver across each other's bow to get in a damaging broadside of cannon fire. A short distance away, the *Pallas* and the *Countess of Scarborough* are firing at each other.

Soon it is evident to Jones that he must try a different strategy. The much older *Bon Homme Richard*'s rotten timbers are being torn to pieces. Cannon balls bounce off the new timbers of the *Serapis* as if they are hitting iron armor.

The American captain decides to bring

his ship next to the *Serapis* so he can board it. When they are side by side, he orders some of his men to lash the two vessels together. Jones jumps from the quarter-deck and swings grappling irons into the other ship's rigging, joining the warships.

Cannon from both vessels continue to fire directly into each other at pointblank range, causing a cloud of smoke to envelop them. Shot and splinters are flying in all directions. Each crew thinks the other is about to board its ship at any moment. Suspense fills the air when Captain Pearson shouts out through the smoke and darkness and asks Captain Jones if he will surrender.

Pearson: Have you struck your colors?

Jones: *(replying in a loud, firm voice)* I have not yet begun to fight!

Narrator 2: Cannon fire from both ships begins again, and the vessels separate. Captain Pearson wants to shoot at the *Bon Homme Richard* from a distance where he can do the most damage, but Captain Jones wants the two warships to come together so that he and his crew can board the *Serapis* and take it by force. With his ship breaking apart under him, this is the only chance to win the battle.

Within an hour, the two vessels become attached once more, and Jones makes an attempt to disable the *Serapis* so that it cannot get away again. Jones, back on the quarter-deck, shouts out orders.

Jones: Fire three cannon against the enemy's mainmast with double-headed shot. That will cripple them.

Dale: Yes, sir.

Jones: Fire two cannon with grapeshot and canister shot to clear its decks of any soldiers firing muskets.

Dale: Sir, some of our officers want you to surrender.

> *"I will not listen to any talk of surrender. I meant it when I said that we had not yet begun to fight."*

Jones: *(angrily)* I will not listen to any talk of surrender. I meant it when I said that we had not yet begun to fight.

Chamillard: *(excitedly)* Sir, the *Alliance* is returning and firing a full broadside of grapeshot into us.

Jones: I knew I could not trust Captain Landais. Shout to him to stop. Maybe he does not recognize our ship.

Chamillard: But it is full moonlight. He must see us.

Jones: Show your position by putting out a lantern at the bow, one at the stern, and one at the middle of the ship, in a horizontal line.

Narrator 2: The signal does not stop Landais, and the *Alliance* returns twice, fires into the *Bon Homme Richard*, and then sails off.

Jones: *(relieved)* At least that traitor Landais has left us. We will deal with him later.

Narrator 2: Fire spreads throughout both warships, and cries of pain rise above the constant cannon fire. Captain Jones is concerned that the flames will spread down to the magazine where the gunpowder kegs are stored. Jones yells to Lieutenant Dale.

Jones: Order some men to bring up the powder kegs from the magazine and throw them into the sea. An explosion would finish us. And keep the men pumping water out of the hold. We must stay afloat at least until we board and capture the *Serapis*.

Dale: Yes, sir. I will go at once.

Jones: *(turning to Lieutenant Chamillard)* Keep our sharpshooters firing at the men on the deck of the *Serapis* and get some of our crew to climb up into the rigging and throw grenades into their open ports.

Chamillard: Yes, sir. I am sure I can find some men for that daring job.

Narrator 2: A brave American volunteers to climb out on the yardarm of the *Bon Homme Richard* that stretches out over the enemy's deck. He carries a bucket of grenades hanging from one arm. He proceeds to shower the grenades onto the *Serapis*. Several fall into the main hatch, where they blow up and cause cartridges of gunpowder near the cannon to explode in rapid succession. This wounds and kills many of the enemy and renders their guns useless.

Meanwhile, the mainmast of the *Serapis* crashes onto the deck after being pounded with double-headed shot by the Americans. The spars and rigging fall with it.

Captain Pearson, his ship in ruins with fire spreading everywhere, hauls down his country's flag himself because his men are afraid of being shot by the sharpshooters from the *Bon Homme Richard*. At this time, the *Pallas* brings the captured *Countess of Scarborough* over to the two warships.

Dale: *(turning to Captain Jones)* Do I have permission to board the enemy's ship, sir?

Jones: Yes, you may take command of the *Serapis*.

Narrator 2: Lieutenant Dale, accompanied by several American sailors, swings onto the quarter-deck of the captured *Serapis* and takes command. Word quickly spreads among the British that their captain has surrendered, and all fighting soon ceases.

This never-to-be-forgotten battle is over. Men lay dead or dying everywhere, and both ships are a wreck. Jones later describes this destruction in his journal:

"A person must have been an eye-witness to form a just idea of the tremendous scene of carnage, wreck, and ruin that everywhere appeared. Humanity cannot but recoil from the prospect of such finished horror, and lament that war should produce such fatal consequences."

Narrator 1: It is soon discovered that the *Bon Homme Richard* cannot be saved. Captain Jones moves all his remaining crew and wounded to the *Serapis*. The Americans make one last attempt to save the noble vessel, but the task is hopeless.

At ten o'clock the next night, the *Bon Homme Richard* sinks to the depths of the sea, carrying the bodies of the dead crew who so bravely gave their lives for the freedom of the new nation across the ocean.

Resource Activities

True or False?

1. John Paul Jones refused to assume command of the *Ranger* because it was such a slow ship.

2. The French king Louis XVI at first refused to listen to Jones's request for a warship.

3. Jones was given an American crew to handle his new ship, the *Duc de Duras.*

4. Jones renamed the *Duc de Duras* the *Bon Homme Richard* in honor of Benjamin Franklin and his book of proverbs.

5. Jones and the *Bon Homme Richard* left France alone to capture British ships.

6. Jones planned to attack and destroy the Scottish town of Leith.

7. Jones planned to deliver the ransom letter in person to the mayor of Leith.

8. Several of Jones's eighteen-pound cannon burst in the battle with the *Serapis,* but the rest were able to be used.

9. In the midst of intense fighting, Jones joined his men on deck to give them courage and brave the battle with them.

10. The *Alliance,* commanded by Captain Landais, helped to cripple the British ship *Serapis.*

Do You Remember?

1. What advice did Benjamin Franklin give John Paul Jones?

2. What happened to the ships that were to accompany the *Bon Homme Richard* and Jones in his quest for British ships in English waters?

3. How did Jones survey the vessels lying at anchor in the harbor of Leith?

4. How did Captain Richard Pearson handle the ships under his command once he spotted Jones's squadron?

5. What helped Jones against the *Serapis* that had hurt him off the coast of Leith?

6. What almost destroyed the *Bon Homme Richard* and lost the battle for Jones?

7. Why did Jones decide to maneuver the *Bon Homme Richard* so that his crew could board the *Serapis*?

8. What was Jones's reply when Captain Pearson asked him if he was surrendering?

9. Why, in the midst of the battle, did Jones order his men to throw the stored gunpowder kegs into the sea?

10. Why did Captain Pearson surrender, especially if the *Bon Homme Richard* was practically helpless?

What Do You Think?

1. John Paul Jones refused to take command of the defeated English warship that was first offered to him in France. Was this a wise decision?

2. The *Duc de Duras* was an old vessel greatly in need of repair. Why did Jones accept command of it so readily?

3. Why did Jones neglect to test or replace the old eighteen-pound cannon if he doubted their worth?

4. Why did Jones allow Captain Landais to be part of his squadron?

5. Why did Jones choose the port of Leith to attack?

6. Jones was eager to challenge the *Serapis.* Why did he prefer this to destroying merchant ships?

7. After the eighteen-pounders burst on the *Bon Homme Richard*, Jones flew into action. What do his actions tell you of his character?

8. Captain Richard Pearson asked Jones if he had struck his colors. What did he mean?

9. Jones signaled to Captain Landais after the *Alliance* fired at the *Bon Homme Richard*. Why?

10. Why did Jones let the *Bon Homme Richard* sink?

From the Historical Perspective

1. John Paul Jones harassed the British coastline. While he longed to enter into battle with an English warship, his capture of British merchant ships greatly aided the American war effort. Why?

2. Why was it more difficult to establish a Continental Navy than the Continental Army?

3. Why were so many naval commands given to French officers? Why did foreigners receive commands at all?

Further Activities

1. John Paul Jones was able to recruit more American sailors for his crew because of an exchange of prisoners between England and the United States. Exchanges of prisoners have occurred quite regularly throughout history. Research a few of the major wars in history and the exchange of prisoners that occurred during those wars. Also research any current exchanges of prisoners, especially in the Middle East and Central America. Why do exchanges occur? Do they have an effect on the war, on the people fighting the war, and on the political process?

2. Jones ordered his men to signal Captain Landais to stop firing at an ally ship. Research the various signals used by vessels in wartime and in peacetime.

3. Design a diorama or make a model of the fight between the *Bon Homme Richard* and the *Serapis*. Include the *Alliance* firing on the *Bon Homme Richard* and the lanterns hung to mark the latter's position.

CHAPTER SEVEN

SLAVES FOR FREEDOM

Historical Overview

In 1775, there were approximately two million people living in the American Colonies and lands of the New World claimed by England. Historians estimate that as many as a half a million were black people. While some blacks were free, the majority were slaves. In the North, slaves were used mainly to help with chores around the house. In the South, where the majority of slaves lived, they worked the fields of the great plantations. The slave trade was a prosperous business, and thousands of black people were taken from their homes in Africa and brought across the sea under horrible conditions.

As more and more colonists condemned the practice of selling and owning other human beings, laws gradually were passed that limited the rights of slave owners and even forbade slavery in some areas. But slavery was not abolished during the Revolutionary War period.

Some slaves won their freedom after years of loyal service. Others were freed according to terms in their masters' wills. Still others obtained their freedom by serving in the Revolutionary War. At first the colonists decreed that blacks could not fight or bear arms. The colonists feared that if the blacks possessed arms, they might use them against their masters and organize their own revolution. The British recognized this opportunity and offered any

slave freedom in return for joining the Redcoats. Many slaves readily accepted the British offer, especially since England seemed more likely to win the war.

When the colonists saw how successful the British were at recruiting blacks, they also began to open their ranks to black recruits. At first blacks were not allowed to carry weapons. They were assigned other duties, such as drummer, fifer, and medical orderly. This eventually changed, and blacks later served in all capacities in the Revolution. Most slaves needed their masters' permission to join the army. Some masters sent their slaves in their place. Two all-black units were formed—the First Rhode Island Regiment and the Bucks of America. Throughout the war, many free blacks, slaves, and ex-slaves performed great feats of daring and courage.

Because of their social position, slaves had little opportunity to learn to read and write. As a result, few left records of their exploits. There was one slave, however, whose owners recognized her abilities and encouraged her to learn. This young girl, Phillis Wheatley, became the first black person to express how it felt to be a slave involved in a revolution fought by whites seeking their freedom. Her poetry was well received and admired by many people, including George Washington.

Today, as scholars and historians review the countless recorded incidents of the American Revolution, more and more information is being unearthed about the valuable contributions made by blacks. Black people were especially helpful in the dangerous task of spying. Death was the punishment if a spy was caught and convicted. The British trusted blacks who claimed to be escaping slavery. This made it a little easier for the black patriot spy. One such black spy was a slave named James Armistead. He managed to enter the camp of the British general Benedict Arnold and pass important information back to the rebels.

Arnold was hated by every patriot. He had been an officer in the Continental Army, leading his men to victory on several occasions. Unfortunately, Arnold did not feel he had been justly honored. This attitude led to resentment and retaliation. Arnold became a spy against the Americans and betrayed the well-supplied and important fort at West Point on the Hudson River in New York. Patriot soldiers discovered Arnold's betrayal when they stopped and questioned Major John André, a British officer. They found, in André's stockings, a secret communication from Arnold to the British explaining his plan to give them West Point. André was tried for spying, convicted, and hanged. Arnold escaped. The British gladly accepted him into their ranks and promoted him to general.

By the 1780s, the war had moved to the South. General Charles Cornwallis was the chief commander of the British forces there. Cornwallis was determined to defeat the rebel forces, particularly those of George Washington, and to end the war. General Arnold was the other ranking British general in the South. Cornwallis ordered his men to lay waste the surrounding countryside. This would eliminate the possibility of the rebel forces resupplying themselves.

Washington was just as determined to destroy Cornwallis, especially since he had the aid of the Comte de Rochambeau and the French Army. James Armistead was sent to spy on Arnold and Cornwallis. His information helped General Washington and the Marquis de Lafayette make their

plans to defeat General Cornwallis. While the French fleet under Admiral de Grasse blocked the British from receiving aid or exiting by sea at Yorktown, Armistead's land reports contributed to Cornwallis's defeat at Yorktown and the end of the Revolution.

Phillis Wheatley:
The Mother of American Poetry

Characters

Phillis Wheatley — a black slave who lives in Massachusetts

John Wheatley — a prosperous Boston tailor

Susannah Wheatley — the wife of John Wheatley

Mary Wheatley — the daughter of John and Susannah Wheatley

Introduction

Narrator 1: Phillis Wheatley was born in 1754, probably in Gambia in western Africa, an area that was populated mostly by Moslems, who had a written language. Phillis's exposure to some form of literature at an early age might have accounted for her interest in reading and writing and her natural ability to put her feelings and thoughts into poetry.

Phillis certainly had the capacity and the desire to learn. When she was purchased as a slave by the Wheatley family in Boston, the Wheatleys quickly realized that Phillis was bright and curious. It was not long before she was being educated by the Wheatleys' daughter, Mary, and writing her own poems. She went on to become the first black person, the first slave, and the second woman to publish a book of poems in America and is considered the first truly American poet.

Act I, Scene 1

Narrator 2: The Wheatley home in Boston in 1761. Susannah Wheatley, the mistress of the house, has just returned from the slave market, where she bought a seven-year-old African girl for the household. Susannah has been looking for a young slave to replace some of her older servants. She also wants a companion to care for her in her old age. Susannah sends the young slave girl to the servants' quarters to be bathed, clothed, and fed. She enters the parlor where her husband and daughter are reading before the fire to tell them of her recent purchase.

Susannah Wheatley: I found a new girl in the slave market today.

Mary Wheatley: (*looking up from her book*) How old is she?

Susannah: About seven years old, I think.

Mary: Oh, good! Mother, may I name her?

Susannah: Yes, my dear, you may.

Mary: I have always liked the name Phillis. I think Phillis Wheatley goes well together. Don't you, Father?

John Wheatley: Yes, Mary, it does. (*turning to his wife*) Is she healthy?

Susannah: Not in appearance. She is very thin and obviously suffering from the

long trip from Africa. The conditions on slave ships are so terrible. It is a wonder that any of them make it here alive. Just the extreme change of climate is enough to do them in. She was naked except for a dirty piece of carpet wrapped around her. She also recently lost her front teeth. That is why I think she is about seven years old.

John: Why did you choose her if she is not healthy? We do not need a sick servant who is unable to do any work.

Susannah: It was the intelligent expression on her face that attracted me to her. She had such a thoughtful look, different from that of the other Africans on the block with her.

Mary: I am anxious to meet Phillis.

Susannah: You may when she has rested.

The poor girl is frightened and exhausted.

Narrator 2: Mary impatiently returns to the book she is reading while her parents continue to discuss other household matters.

Act I, Scene 2

Narrator 1: The Wheatley home sixteen months later. Susannah Wheatley soon realizes that she has bought an extraordinary girl with a sharp mind. Phillis is not trained as a domestic as it was first intended, and she is not allowed to associate with the other servants in the household. She is kept constantly in the company of her mistress and Mary. Susannah, Mary, and Phillis are spending a quiet afternoon in the library.

Susannah: Phillis, are you cold? I am worried about the effect of this damp weather on your delicate health.

Phillis Wheatley: No, Mistress Wheatley. The wool shawl you gave me and the fire are keeping me plenty warm.

Susannah: I am still amazed at how well you speak English. You have only been with us sixteen months!

Mary: (*proudly looking at her pupil, who lowers her head humbly*) And she can read well, too.

Susannah: I know. I told our neighbors that Phillis could read the sacred writings of the Bible, but they did not believe me. I had to bring them in and prove it to them. They were astonished.

Mary: She also has been learning to write since I had her put the alphabet on the wall with a piece of chalk. Now we practice every day with chalk or charcoal.

Susannah: What subjects are you learning now, Phillis?

Phillis: Mary has started to teach me about astronomy, geography, and literature. I want to learn about everything.

Susannah: Why is that?

Phillis: I am just curious, I guess.

Susannah: That's a good enough reason. What do you enjoy learning the most?

Phillis: I like words and the way different ones sound. I like to put them together so that they have special meaning.

Susannah: Maybe someday you will write poetry.

Phillis: What is poetry?

Susannah: You will learn, Phillis. You will learn.

Narrator 2: The two girls continue studying as Susannah sits watching them contently, happy that she chose to bring this bright young girl into her house.

Phillis's poor health does not keep her from her studies, which continue over the years under the direction of Mary and some of her friends. When she is fourteen years old, Phillis writes her first poem—"To the University of Cambridge"—in which she advises disobedient college boys to avoid sin and follow Christ. Phillis continues to write poems, and she soon becomes widely known throughout America and Europe.

Act I, Scene 3

Narrator 1: The Wheatley home on a Sunday afternoon in August 1772. The cold, damp New England weather has affected Phillis's fragile health. She has asthma, and to help her condition, the Wheatleys send her to the country during the week. She returns to the city to spend every Sunday with the family. Over dinner, John, Susannah, and Mary Wheatley discuss with

Phillis the progress of her studies and her future.

John: Phillis, Mary has told me that you have been learning Latin. How have you done with it?

Phillis: Very well, sir. I have been fortunate to have tutors like Mary and her friends who have been able to teach me so many subjects.

John: What subjects have you been studying and reading about lately?

Phillis: I have been studying Christian scripture, ancient history, and mythology.

John: You obviously love to learn. What do you enjoy the most?

Phillis: I like to read the classics, expecially Virgil, Ovid, and Horace. I also have enjoyed the writings of Milton, Gray, Addison, and Isaac Watts. I like the literature of Pope very much, and I especially love his translation of Homer.

John: Why is that?

Phillis: I use his meter and rhyme in most of my verse when I write poetry.

John: (*very impressed*) You are getting the equal of a Harvard education. (*turning to his daughter*) Mary, I am pleased with the quality and the quantity of education you have given Phillis. Her poetry shows your efforts.

Mary: Thank you, Father. I must admit that she has learned much on her own.

Susannah: I have placed a light and writing material on a table beside Phillis's bed in case she should have any thoughts at night. That way she can write them down without having to get up and go to her desk in the cold. Her health is so delicate.

Phillis: Thank you, Mistress Wheatley. I often have ideas that would flee by dawn if I were not to write them down before I rose.

> *"I like the way different words sound. I like to put them together so that they have special meaning."*

John: You must continue to put your thoughts on paper. You received much fame for the poem you wrote in memory of the Reverend George Whitefield, who preached that Christ was the savior of both blacks and whites. It has even been read in Europe. Last year, Dr. Benjamin Rush wrote about you in his *Address Upon Slave-Keeping*. He said that there was an eighteen-year-old black girl who has been in this country about eleven years and whose talents and accomplishments have done honor to her as a female and also to human nature. That was a strong compliment from so distinguished a person.

Phillis: Yes, sir. I was pleased to read that.

John: What poem are you writing now?

Phillis: I have been following the political events in the Colonies with great enthusiasm. I have written a poem that makes a statement about the black patriot's position.

John: How are you going to present this noble and worthy statement?

Phillis: This month, the earl of Dartmouth was appointed as secretary of state for our Colonies. This is a good sign for the end of British tyranny in America. The earl was a good friend of the Reverend Whitefield, who, as you know, was a friend of blacks. He also is friendly with the countess of Huntington, who is against slavery. I want to welcome the earl with a message from patriotic blacks in our land.

John: May we hear this new poem of yours?

Susannah: Yes, Phillis, read your poem to us.

Phillis: (*proudly*) I will be happy to read it to you.

Narrator 2: Phillis goes to her room to

get her recently completed poem. She returns shortly to stand before her master and mistress and their daughter to read it out loud.

Phillis: I greet the earl of Dartmouth with my opening lines:
> "Hail, happy day, when smiling like the
>   morn,
> Fair freedom rose New-England to adorn."

I then go on:
> "No more America, in mournful strain
> Of wrongs, and grievance unredress'd
>   complain,
> No longer shall thou dread the iron chain,
> Which wanton Tyranny with lawless hand
> Had made, and with it meant t'enslave the
>   land."

the key words in those lines are "America," "Tyranny," and "t'enslave." They lead to the next stanza, which makes a statement of one side of black patriotism:
> "Should you, my lord, while you peruse
>   my song,
> Wonder from whence my love of Freedom
>   sprung,
> Whence flow these wishes for the common
>   good,
> By feeling hearts alone best understood,
> I, young in life, by seeming cruel fate
> Was snatch'd from Afric's fancy'd happy
>   seat:
> What pangs excruciating must molest,
> What sorrows labour in my parent's
>   breast?
> Steel'd was that soul and by no misery
>   mov'd
> That from a father seiz'd his babe belov'd:"

And I end with:
> "Such, such my case. And can I then but
>   pray
> Others may never feel tyrannic sway?"

Narrator 2: John, Susannah, and Mary applaud the performance. Phillis beams with pride and pleasure at the approval of her patrons.

John: That was moving, Phillis. I am sure the earl will be impressed by your efforts and affected by your message. Have you ever thought to put your poems into a book? I think that such a venture would meet with much success. Your poems are individually so widely read and admired now.

Phillis: Yes, sir. I have wanted to publish my poems collectively. I have already put together a manuscript of almost forty poems. All I need now is one to begin the book—an ode that will thank you for all you have given to me and a statement that declares that I am a black poet.

John: I am very happy to hear that you have already compiled your poems into a manuscript for publication. When you have completed the beginning ode, give them all to me, and I will send the manuscript to my friend, Archibald Bell, the London bookseller.

Phillis: (*with tears in her eyes*) Thank you again, sir. I am so grateful for all your support.

Susannah: We are grateful to you, Phillis. You have enriched our lives so much, and your poetry will continue to enrich and influence the lives of many generations to come in our young, promising land.

Narrator 1: John Wheatley sends Phillis's manuscript to England. Archibald Bell shows the poems to the countess of Huntington, and she is very pleased with them. She asks if Phillis is a real person. The countess also is pleased that the book is dedicated to her. She requests that a picture of Phillis be engraved on the frontispiece of the book. Phillis has her friend and fellow slave Scipio Moorhead paint a portrait of her, and it is sent to London to be engraved.

Phillis travels to London for a change of climate to help her health and also to be there in person the day the volume comes off the press. She makes many friends in England, including Benjamin Franklin, who is quite impressed with her.

Phillis's book is a great success in America and England, and she continues to write more poems. She even writes one to George Washington, who, in return, invites her to visit him. By the time of her death in 1784 at the age of thirty-one, Phillis has written more than seventy poems about freedom, God, and being black in a white revolution. Phillis Wheatley is truly the mother of American poetry.

James Armistead:
Master Spy of
the American Revolution

Characters

Marquis de Lafayette — a young French nobleman who came to America to volunteer his services to the Continental Army

George Washington — the commander of the Continental Army

James Armistead — a twenty-one-year-old black slave from Virginia

Introduction

Narrator 1: In 1781, General George Washington sent a small force of about twelve hundred soldiers south under the command of the Marquis de Lafayette. Their task was to stop the British, who had invaded Virginia. The twenty-three-year-old Frenchman had come to America four years earlier as a volunteer to help the Americans fight for freedom. This was his first chance to lead an army against the English.

When General Lafayette arrived in Virginia, he faced many problems. The local farmers hid their horses and equipment so that Lafayette could not seize them for his own use against the British. The farmers also refused to sell food to the French general to feed his army.

General Lafayette soon discovered that he had not one but two British armies to fight. One was commanded by the American traitor General Benedict Arnold, and the other was under General Lord Charles Cornwallis. Both of these armies had well-trained soldiers and thousands of horses stolen from Virginia farmers.

The British had already burned the capital at Richmond. They also had destroyed supplies of arms and food, as well as warehouses of tobacco, a valuable crop used for trading. The young French general had a difficult task ahead of him, and he was forced to use whatever means were necessary to rid Virginia of the enemy.

Act I, Scene 1

Narrator 2: General Washington's headquarters in April 1781. General Lafayette is conferring with Washington on how to halt British raiders from looting and burning their way through Virginia. Lafayette enters the American leader's library. Washington rises to greet him and shakes his hand.

George Washington: Welcome, my friend. I am anxious to hear of your progress in Virginia. Come and have a seat by the fire.

Marquis de Lafayette: Thank you, sir. I am afraid that all is not going well. I have encountered more difficulties than I thought I would.

Narrator 2: Washington and Lafayette sit facing each other in wing-backed chairs in front of the fireplace.

Washington: What difficulties do you talk of?

Lafayette: Governor Jefferson warned me that Virginia was a state of "mild laws and a people not used to prompt obedience." He was right.

Washington: I know that Virginians have their own way of doing things.

Lafayette: I have tried to get horses for my troops from the Virginia farmers, but they have hid them and their wagons.

Washington: They probably want to save what horses they have left for farm work because the British have already stolen so many of them for their own troops.

Lafayette: My soldiers also are hungry. The farmers will not sell us their meat and grain. They refuse to exchange their produce for American paper money because they claim it is almost worthless.

Washington: That has been a problem with which we all have had to deal.

Lafayette: I have had to contend with two British armies of well-trained troops. Both have been moving swiftly through the state, burning and looting everywhere they go. They have burned Richmond and many

James Armistead has volunteered to serve the Americans as a soldier and spy.

warehouses full of tobacco, weapons, and food. They have even chased many members of the Virginia legislature across the state.

Washington: I heard that Governor Jefferson just barely escaped being captured and that he resigned from office.

Lafayette: The government of Virginia has no power. The British can easily invade such a land.

Washington: Especially with leaders such as the traitor Benedict Arnold and General Cornwallis.

Lafayette: I refuse to give up, though. Do you have any advice for me?

Washington: Yes. Have your soldiers keep watch over every movement the British make. But do not get too close. You are not strong enough to win a battle just yet. Send spies into their camps. I need all the information I can get.

Lafayette: Where can I get more help?

Washington: Recruit black troops. You should be able to enlist several hundred. They could help you find more horses for your soldiers.

Lafayette: I will begin at once. The next time we meet, I will have better news to report to you.

Narrator 2: Washington smiles as the determined young Frenchman leaves the room.

Act I, Scene 2

Narrator 1: Lafayette's headquarters one week later. The general interviews a black slave named James Armistead. He has volunteered to serve the Americans as a soldier and spy. Armistead stands at attention before Lafayette.

Lafayette: What is your name?

James Armistead: James, sir.

Lafayette: And your last name?

Armistead: Armistead, after my master, William Armistead.

Lafayette: Where are you from?

Armistead: My master's farm near the town of Williamsburg in New Kent County.

Lafayette: How old are you?

Armistead: Twenty-one years old, sir.

Lafayette: Why did you come to our camp?

Armistead: I asked my master for permission to enlist under you, General Lafayette.

Lafayette: Why me?

Armistead: Your fame has spread throughout Virginia, and I have heard that you need recruits. I asked my master if I could enlist under you, and he granted me permission. You are fighting to help America become free from British rule, and I, too, want my freedom someday.

Lafayette: (*impressed by the slave's sincerity*) Are you willing to risk your life as a spy for us in the British camp of Benedict Arnold?

Armistead: Yes, sir.

Lafayette: You must understand that I cannot promise you your freedom, even if you do this for us. Only your master or a decree from the General Assembly of Virginia can declare you a free man.

Armistead: I know, sir. I am willing to take my chances.

Lafayette: I can see that you are a brave and intelligent young man. I think you will be loyal to the Americans and a good spy.

Armistead: Thank you, sir.

Lafayette: I want you to make your way to the headquarters of our enemy, Benedict Arnold. Offer him your services. Tell him you want to earn your freedom. I am sure he will believe you. Volunteer to serve his officers as a guide on the country roads. Learn all that you can about the British and follow their every movement. Then report everything that you see and hear to me as often as possible.

Armistead: Yes, sir.

Lafayette: You may leave today. We have no time to waste.

Narrator 2: Armistead leaves the American camp and makes his way to Arnold's headquarters. He soon wins the confidence of the British and sends reports back to Lafayette almost every day. Some of this secret information is used by the Americans, who sneak into the British camp and nearly capture General Arnold himself. Even after this incident, the British continue to trust Armistead.

Act I, Scene 3

Narrator 1: George Washington's headquarters in July 1781. Lafayette reports his progress spying on the British in Virginia. The two generals stroll about the camp on the warm summer evening discussing what has happened since their last meeting.

General Arnold has left Virginia, returning to the North. Armistead is now serving at the headquarters of General Cornwallis.

Washington: So Benedict Arnold has left Virginia. Now you have only one British general with whom to contend, and a capable and cautious general at that. Have your spies had any success with Lord Cornwallis?

Lafayette: I have a very loyal and able black slave, James Armistead, who has volunteered his services as a spy against the British. He sent me a great deal of information when he was in the headquarters of

General Arnold.

Washington: Is he now with Lord Cornwallis?

Lafayette: Yes, but he is having a much more difficult time obtaining secret reports from General Cornwallis. His lordship is so careful with his maps and orders that my spy tells me that he sometimes cannot get at them.

Washington: Have you been able to follow the British through Virginia?

Lafayette: I have often had to guess at the movement of the enemy. They seem to travel as fast as the wind. They try to keep out of our reach. I have to admit that I am devilishly afraid of this cautious and intelligent general.

Washington: You must not lose track of him.

Lafayette: Our small army followed a few miles behind Cornwallis when he marched west through Virginia to the Blue Ridge Mountains and then back to the coast. He knew we were behind him, but I told my men that we were chasing them. This lifted their morale.

Washington: That was clever of you. Do you think this James Armistead will be able to get much information to you? How much is he trusted by Lord Cornwallis?

Lafayette: James Armistead spends a lot of time in the tent of Cornwallis. He also serves the general and his officers their food and drink. They would not allow his presence at meals if he were not trusted. He pretends not to understand their plans.

Washington: How does he get word to you?

Lafayette: He tells what he has overheard to other black men in the camp who have the liberty to come and go. They bring me the secret information a couple of hours later.

Washington: Where is Cornwallis now?

Lafayette: He and his army have moved to the city of Portsmouth near Chesapeake Bay. James Armistead tells me that a fleet of British sailing ships is anchored in the harbor. The ships seem ready to carry the enemy troops to a new location, but I have received no news that Cornwallis and his men have sailed.

Washington: Keep reporting all your news to me. I am anxious to keep track of Lord Cornwallis. His capture would contribute greatly to the success of our war efforts.

Lafayette: With the help of my trustworthy spy, I am sure we will be victorious.

Narrator 2: Lafayette leaves to return to his camp in Virginia. He wants to be present if any critical news should arrive from his spy and scouts.

Act I, Scene 4

Narrator 1: Lafayette's headquarters. In early August, Armistead himself reports to the young French general.

Lafayette: (*surprised*) I am glad to see you, James. But why have you come in person?

Armistead: General Cornwallis has sailed with his army from Portsmouth.

Lafayette: Do you have any other information?

Armistead: I could not find out where they are going.

Lafayette: I will send scouts to find out his destination. I must notify General Washington at once. You have served your country and me well. We are grateful to you for your service and devotion to the American fight for liberty. I will do whatever I can to assist you in your quest for freedom.

Armistead: Thank you, sir. When the war is over, I plan to petition the General Assembly of Virginia to declare me a free man.

Lafayette: Let us hope this war will be over soon.

Narrator 2: It is not long before Lafayette learns from his scouts that General Cornwallis and his army have landed at Yorktown, a small port on the York River near the Chesapeake Bay. This news is reported to General Washington, who tells Lafayette and his army to keep the British from leaving the port.

Meanwhile, General Washington and his troops, along with the French troops under the Comte de Rochambeau, march south to Yorktown. Admiral de Grasse and his French fleet sail to the Chesapeake Bay. By September, Cornwallis is surrounded by American and French troops. On October 19, after ten days of being bombarded by cannon, General Cornwallis surrenders. The final battle of the American Revolution is over.

One year after the peace treaty is signed by the United States and Great Britain, General Lafayette writes a certificate praising the loyalty and wisdom of James Armistead, who played such an important role in America's fight for freedom.

Armistead sends this certificate along with a petition to declare him free to the General Assembly of Virginia. The assembly agrees to pay his master, William Armistead, a fair price for his freedom. In appreciation for the trust and assistance given to him by General Lafayette, Armistead changes his name to James Armistead Lafayette.

> *"They would not allow his presence if he were not trusted. He pretends not to understand their plans."*

Resource Activities

True or False?

Phillis Wheatley

1. Phillis Wheatley was born on a southern plantation and then sold to the Wheatley family of Boston.
2. Susannah and Mary Wheatley educated Phillis over the objections of John Wheatley.
3. Phillis enjoyed learning and appreciated the Wheatleys' continued interest in her progress.
4. For many years, Phillis had difficulty getting her poems read and accepted by people other than the Wheatleys' friends and associates.

James Armistead

5. In March 1781, General George Washington and the Marquis de Lafayette headed south to fight the British troops invading Virginia.
6. The Virginians supplied Lafayette and his troops with horses and fresh supplies of food.
7. James Armistead wanted to fight to free America from England and volunteered to serve in the Continental Army.
8. Lafayette promised Armistead his freedom if he served the Continental Army well.
9. Armistead's first spying assignment was to obtain a position in General Charles Cornwallis's headquarters.
10. Armistead's spy ring was so unorganized that it took one to two days for information to reach Lafayette.

Do You Remember?

Phillis Wheatley

1. Why did Susannah Wheatley buy Phillis?
2. Which member of the Wheatley family spent the most time training Phillis?
3. How did John Wheatley help Phillis get her book published?
4. Why did Phillis Wheatley dedicate her first book of poems to the countess of Huntington?

James Armistead

5. Who were the two British generals commanding the British troops in Virginia?
6. What did George Washington say was the best strategy to use against the British in Virginia?
7. How did James Armistead, a slave, come to serve under the Marquis de Lafayette?
8. How did Armistead come to serve General Charles Cornwallis?
9. How did General Benedict Arnold and General Cornwallis differ according to Armistead?
10. To whom did Armistead send his request for freedom?

What Do You Think?

Phillis Wheatley

1. What do you think was the Wheatley family's position on slavery?
2. Why did studying a variety of topics help Phillis Wheatley become a better writer?
3. Why did John Wheatley choose an English bookseller, and not an American one, to publish Phillis's first book?
4. Do you think Phillis's presence in England when her book was published contributed to its success?

James Armistead

5. Why did the British steal American horses and destroy colonists' food and ammunition

supplies?

6. Why was American paper money considered worthless?

7. Why did George Washington forbid Lafayette to fight Cornwallis? What other reason, besides the size of Lafayette's force, might have influenced Washington's decision?

8. How did James Armistead manage to win Benedict Arnold's confidence so easily?

9. Why did General Charles Cornwallis guard his maps and military plans?

10. General Cornwallis was a determined and clever British military commander. Why did he surrender to General Washington?

From the Historical Perspective

1. Why did the American Revolution lead many colonists, especially in the North, to reconsider their position on slavery?

2. Why did the American leaders hesitate to recruit blacks for the Continental Army?

3. While there were many traitors during the American Revolution, Benedict Arnold's name is the one remembered with the most disgust. Why has his accomplice, Major John André, not received the same treatment?

Further Activities

1. Research the processes and routes used by slave traders to capture and bring people to the American Colonies to sell as slaves.

2. Copy or draw a map of the original thirteen American colonies. Shade in those colonies where slavery was widely accepted and practiced, the first states to abolish slavery (pencil in the date), and the states that limited the rights of slave owners.

3. Research other black Americans who fought for or helped the colonists during the Revolution. You may wish to consider Crispus Attucks, James Forten, or Agrippa Hull.

4. Not all blacks in the Colonies were slaves or freed slaves. Many were free from birth, and several figured prominently in American history. Research the lives and deeds of Paul Cuffee and Benjamin Banneker.

CHAPTER EIGHT

THE QUEST FOR NATIONAL UNITY

Historical Overview

The American patriots fought their last great battle for freedom at Yorktown, Virginia. There were other skirmishes after Yorktown, but the surrender on October 17, 1781, of British general Charles Cornwallis to American general George Washington signaled the official end of the American Revolution.

Americans in all thirteen states rejoiced. The hardships and sorrows of the war had brought victory. They now were free from the harsh laws and unjust taxes of a distant country. But as the months and years following Cornwallis's surrender passed, Americans began to realize that their difficulties were not over. The war had been a very costly struggle for freedom. To pay for the war, Congress had borrowed millions in foreign currency, mostly at high interest rates. Congress also had established the Continental Army and owed many soldiers back pay.

During the war, business trade had almost stopped, thereby eliminating needed revenue. After the war, Britain forbade its other colonies to trade with the United States. This was a tremendous financial blow for American merchants. Britain also imposed restrictive laws on exporting and importing goods. Creditors, especially for-eign creditors, accepted only coins as payment. Consequently, gold and silver coins became increasingly scarce.

Congress had authorized paper money to be printed during the war, but this money was not backed by gold or silver to secure its financial worth. As a result, some creditors, especially merchants, refused to accept this money, which they considered worthless. To resolve this problem, the states agreed to back the American currency. However, the states also owed millions in war debts. They could not pay their own bills, let alone honor Congress's debts.

States then began issuing their own paper currency. But often one state did not honor the paper money of another state, and trade across state borders became almost impossible. The main reason for this desperate situation was Congress's lack of power over the states. Each state had laws that allowed it to raise funds. For example, a state could tax its citizens and could levy taxes on trade goods. Congress, however, could not tax unless it had the full approval of the states. The reason for this situation is easily understood. The Americans were fighting to free themselves from a government they considered unjust. They certainly did not want to create another government with the same type of powers.

To ease Congress's debt problems, four states (Virginia, New York, Massachusetts, and Connecticut) agreed to give Congress the land they claimed northwest of the Ohio River across to the Mississippi River. The states reasoned that Congress could sell the land for hard coin and use the income to pay some of its debts. Under the Land Ordinance of 1785, this territory, known as the Northwest Territory, was divided into townships six miles square. Each township was further subdivided into one-mile-square sections that were sold for $640 each. People in all thirteen states hoped this new settlement would provide the needed funds to set the United States on its way to becoming a nation recognized by other nations, both politically and economically.

The Land Ordinance of 1785 worked to some extent. Settlers moved westward and bought land. But the problem of debt still remained. In western Massachusetts, farmers found themselves in serious financial difficulties. During the war, their goods had been in great demand. As a result, they had borrowed money to buy equipment and other supplies to meet the demand. After the war, the demand dropped, but the debt remained. Almost everyone owed money. State governments acted to resolve the situation. They raised taxes to obtain revenue. They also decreed that creditors could take the property of persons who could not pay their debts. The courts were ordered to settle cases between debtors and creditors.

Riots broke out as people, many of whom had staunchly supported the patriots and served in the army under terrible conditions, saw their homes, property, equipment, and livestock taken by creditors. Most were helpless to do anything.

In 1786, Daniel Shays, a former captain in the Continental Army, led a group of men against the system and, for a time, successfully prevented courts in western Massachusetts from meeting and deciding the fate of debtors. The Massachusetts legislature raised an army that defeated Shays and his men, but Massachusetts citizens learned a valuable lesson. At the next elections, new officials were put into office who treated creditors and debtors more fairly.

Shays's Rebellion had a national affect. It proved the need for a stronger Congress—one that could act on behalf of the states and not allow individuals or individual states to lead their own rebellions. The people sought a Congress that could help protect the rights of all, whether they be personal, economic, or religious.

Shays's Rebellion

Characters

Daniel Shays — a Revolutionary War veteran

Abigail Shays — Daniel's wife

Job Shattuck — a veteran of the French and Indian War and the Revolutionary War

Samuel Ely — a preacher and veteran of the Revolutionary War

Luke Day — a veteran of the Revolutionary War and a poor farmer

William Conkey — a good friend of Daniel Shays and the owner of a tavern in Pelham

Rufus Putnam — an old friend and former commander of Daniel Shays during the Revolutionary War

Soldier — a messenger from General Shepard

Messenger — a messenger from General Lincoln

Introduction

Narrator 1: After the British surrender at Yorktown, Virginia, on October 17, 1781, Massachusetts veterans of the Continental Army returned to their homes for a well-earned rest. The soldiers were happy to be reunited with their families and were anxious to resume work on their farms. But the returning soldiers were disappointed with the system of government that had been organized while they were at war. Only people who had enough property could qualify as representatives in one of the two legislative chambers. This system gave more control to rich merchants and little representation to poor farmers. Heavy taxes were created by the states to pay back the millions of dollars that had been borrowed to finance war costs.

Farmers were especially hard hit because they were in debt to merchants for money borrowed during the war to buy land, livestock, and equipment. Veterans often were faced with going to jail or having their property confiscated because they could not pay the high taxes or the money they owed to the merchants. To discuss their problems and frustrations, the discouraged men organized county conventions. These were made up of representatives from the towns in each county.

The first county convention took place in Hampshire County in the town of Hadley on February 11, 1782. The people at this convention listed high taxes and the harsh court judgments on poor debtors as their main complaints. They asked the Massachusetts legislature, called the General Court, to issue paper money to help farmers in debt and to allow personal property to be used to pay off debts and taxes. The legislature ignored the petitions from the convention.

Since the General Court would not act on their requests, several delegates from the convention decided that they should band together to prevent the judges from holding court and sentencing to jail more poor farmers who could not pay their debts. They said they were following a precedent set during the Revolution when the courts were closed to protect rebelling colonists from retaliation by the British.

County conventions continued to be held for several years. They also began to send resolutions to meetings convened in other counties. Continued attempts to change Massachusetts's government were made with no results. The legislature did not consider the conventions legal assemblies and rejected all their petitions. In 1784, the General Court even raised taxes again. The economic condition of the state was bad. Merchants still were impatient for their money, and the poor farmers were angry.

Daniel Shays, a veteran of the Revolution, was an angry delegate from the town of Pelham to the county convention in Hadley in 1782. He had seen some of his friends and neighbors jailed by the strict, unbending courts, and by 1784 he also was in debt. After attending several conventions, he joined the bands of men who formed to prevent judges from holding court.

> *Daniel Shays, a veteran of the Revolution, was an angry delegate from the town of Pelham.*

Act I, Scene 1

Narrator 2: Conkey's Tavern in Pelham, Massachusetts, in 1786. A committee of Hampshire County farmers and some local men are meeting to convince Daniel Shays to lead the growing band of people who are against the oppression of the General Court and stop the court at Springfield from convening. The tavern is a respectable meeting place for the men of the area. The owner, William Conkey, is a close friend of Daniel Shays. The men sit in the front parlor and discuss the situation.

Daniel Shays: Why have you asked me here? I should be home working on my farm. I have a family to feed and debts to pay.

Job Shattuck: Most of us are in the same situation, Daniel. That is why we are all here today. We must do something about the courts. The General Court will not listen to our petitions, so we must stop the judges from opening the courts and handing out more jail sentences to people who cannot pay their debts.

Samuel Ely: (*angrily*) It is about time we had less talk and more action.

Shattuck: That is why we are here, Daniel, to get more action. But first we need a strong leader. You have been chosen to stop the courts from convening in Springfield.

Shays: (*surprised*) Why me? There are so many other men more qualified to be the leader. (*turning to Shattuck*) You, for example, Job.

Shattuck: A younger man than I is needed, and one with a clean record. I had to pay a fine for leading a riot against the silver tax. Remember?

Shays: Yes, I do. What about Luke Day? He is a good speaker and a sensible organizer.

Shattuck: Some men do not like his notions about the Bible. They do not trust his emotional way of being inspired by the sacred scriptures. They fear he will be uncooperative with his fellow men and become a dictator.

Shays: Adam Wheeler would be a good leader.

Ely: Adam was considered, but he has already been accused by the courts of rebellious behavior.

Shays: What qualifications do I have?

Ely: You have been a staunch supporter of our cause from the beginning.

Shays: That is certainly true.

Shattuck: You are widely known from all the conventions you have attended.

Ely: And you are a sympathetic person who uses self-control. You have the spirit and strength of character to lead us, and you are cautious as well.

Shays: (*blushing*) I am overwhelmed by your compliments, but I have kept out of trouble up until now. If I take this command, I will be committing treason. My life will be in danger, and my family's safety will be threatened. I have heard that in August Sheriff Elisha Porter was seen writing down the names of Captain Luke Day and several other rebels when they marched to Northampton to prevent the Courts of Common Pleas and General Sessions from convening.

Shattuck: The fact that your record is clean is one of the reasons we want you as our leader.

Shays: I still hesitate to take on this great responsibility.

William Conkey: Daniel, you are a natural leader. Everyone in Pelham has praised the militia you have drilled here. Your soldiers during the Revolution respected you, and your neighbors admire you now.

Shays: (*again blushing*) Thank you for your kind words, William.

Conkey: I mean them. You will bring honor to Pelham if you take this position.

Shays: It seems that I will be an outcast in my own town if I do not take this command.

Conkey: That, unfortunately, is probably true.

Shays: I had enough of ostracism in 1780 when I sold the sword the Marquis de Lafayette presented to me for my service during the Revolution. Although I needed the money to feed and clothe my family, I was still shunned by my friends and fellow officers. That hurt. But I am no coward either. I will accept the command. I only hope that I can live up to all that you have said of me.

Narrator 2: The men cheer and begin planning the next step in their rebellion. On September 26, 1786, Captain Daniel Shays parades about seven hundred men down Springfield's only street. Major General William Shepard and his army of several hundred men surround the courthouse to protect it. Shepard supplies his men with four hundred muskets and a small cannon he has taken from the arsenal at Springfield.

After making this show of strength, Shays calls a council of his men, who write a petition to the judges. It states that they will withdraw if the judges promise not to jail them for bearing arms. It asks that farmers not be taxed for the cost of the army that was sent against them. The judges reply that they cannot do anything inconsistent with the important duties of their court.

This reply irritates Shays and his men, and they continue to parade around Springfield. Soon Shepard withdraws with his men to the arsenal, and Shays and the rebels occupy the courthouse for a short time as a gesture of defiance. This situation is arranged by both Shepard and Shays so there will be no bloodshed.

> *"I am no coward. I only hope that I can live up to all that you have said of me."*

Act I, Scene 2

Narrator 1: The farmhouse of Daniel Shays in Pelham in early December 1786. Shays is discussing recent events with his wife, Abigail.

Daniel Shays: It makes me furious knowing that while I was parading my men in Springfield, the General Court in Boston passed a Riot Act. Apparently Governor Bowdoin told the legislature that the rebels needed to be punished. He should have recommended legislation that might solve the problems of the poor farmers in debt instead.

Abigail Shays: What exactly is the Riot Act?

Daniel: The act states that if any armed gathering does not break up within an hour after a sheriff reads the Riot Act to them, their property will be taken, they will be whipped publicly, and they will be imprisoned for one year during which time they are to be whipped every three months.

Abigail: *(alarmed)* Daniel, do be careful! That is a harsh act.

Daniel: The senate also suspended habeas corpus.

Abigail: What is habeas corpus?

Daniel: It is a form of protection against unjust imprisonment. A prisoner must be brought before a judge who decides whether or not the prisoner can legally be put into jail.

Abigail: The legislators must be afraid of what you and your men might do.

Daniel: They certainly are. They also gave Governor Bowdoin the power to call out the militia.

Abigail: Have they used the Riot Act yet?

Daniel: Yes. It was read by Sheriff William Greenleaf to about one hundred sixty farmers who marched on the Court of General Sessions that met in Worcester on November 21.

Abigail: Who led that march?

Daniel: Job Shattuck, Adam Wheeler, and Henry Gale. Job was caught two days ago, and he was wounded in the knee. He is now in jail in Boston. Adam and Henry escaped. I have sent word to Adam to meet me in Worcester tomorrow. When he arrives, we are going to begin collecting supplies of arms and ammunition from neighboring towns for our men.

Abigail: What do you plan to do next? The legislature obviously takes your actions seriously.

Daniel: After meeting with the leaders from Worcester, I am going to send out a letter to be circulated throughout western and central Massachusetts.

Abigail: What are you going to say in this letter?

Daniel: I plan to write that the seeds of war have been sown. I will ask every town and village to send us men and supplies. The public must be convinced that we are determined to carry out our plans and that our cause is their cause as well. We need support now, or we will die here. We are all brothers in our fight for justice.

Narrator 2: On December 3, 1786, Captain Shays marches about three hundred fifty men into Worcester. He plans to prevent the Court of Common Pleas from meeting on December 5. The rebels are confronted by a militia led by a Captain Howe and flee to neighboring hills across from the courthouse.

A blizzard strikes on December 4 and continues through the next day. Shays

> *"We need support now, or we will die here. We are all brothers in our fight for justice."*

meets with other rebel leaders, and they decide to send a petition to the General Court asking for the restoration of habeas corpus, the release of Job Shattuck from jail in Boston, and a pardon for everyone who has taken up arms. They also state that they have no intention of overthrowing the state government. The rebel leaders explain that they gathered together to protest because they could not provide for their families or pay their debts. They end by promising to end the rebellion if the entire petition is accepted by the General Court. The rebels then return home to await the legislature's answer. Shays decides he will take up arms again only if the General Court rejects the Worcester Petition.

Act I, Scene 3

Narrator 1: A road near Pelham in January 1787. Daniel Shays meets Rufus Putnam, an old friend and former commander, and they discuss the current situation between the rebels and the state government. The two men greet each other, pull up their horses, and proceed to walk down the road and talk.

Daniel Shays: Rufus, I have not seen you for a long while. How have you been?

Rufus Putnam: I have been well. And you, my old friend?

Shays: I have been active in the rebellion against our unfair court system and state government. I must admit that I have become very nervous.

Putnam: I have heard of your activities, and I am glad to have the chance to talk to you about it. What about this petition you and your friends sent to Boston?

Shays: I have decided that I cannot in

good conscience take up arms again unless the Worcester Petition, as we call it, is refused by the General Court.

Putnam: The legislature will never grant everything you asked for in the petition. They will be giving up too much.

Shays: I am afraid of that.

Putnam: I plead with you to give up. You do not stand a chance against the government officials in Boston or the militia they command. If you do not stop your rebellious actions, you will most certainly be captured and hanged.

Shays: (*nervously*) I have to admit that I am frightened by that possibility.

Putnam: Would you accept a pardon if it were offered to you?

Shays: Yes, I would, without a moment's hesitation.

Narrator 2: After that remark, the two men drop the subject and reminisce about their experiences together during the Revolution. Shays later learns that Governor Bowdoin has rejected the Worcester Petition. On January 24, 1787, Shays and a detachment of eleven hundred men head for the federal arsenal at Springfield, which is filled with a large supply of muskets, cannon, and gunpowder that the rebels need for their army. Major General William Shepard guards the arsenal and takes some of the supplies for his nine hundred men because he was cut off from help by Luke Day's rebels on the west and Eli Parsons's rebels on the north. Shepard sends word to Major General Benjamin Lincoln to send some troops against Shays's men who are advancing on Springfield.

Captain Shays needs help attacking the arsenal, and he sends a message to Luke Day. Day vainly wants all the credit for forcing Shepard to surrender and sends a message back to Shays saying that he cannot send help until January 26. The messenger is caught at a tavern in Springfield, and Shays never gets the message. Shays, thinking that Day's support is on the way, marches to Springfield to confront Shepard's army on Arsenal Hill.

Act I, Scene 4

Narrator 1: Arsenal Hill on January 25, 1787. General Shepard's troops are lined up on the hill in front of the arsenal with a cannon pointed at the road. Captain Shays's men are poorly armed with all sorts of weapons, but they are excited and anxious for action. They march to within two hundred fifty yards of the militia and stop to wait

for Shays's command. General Shepard does not want to order his men to fire on their fellow countrymen. He sends a soldier to plead with Captain Shays.

Shays: What message do you have from General Shepard?
Soldier: The general sends a plea to you to stop your march on the arsenal. He also wishes to know what you want.
Shays: (*in a determined voice*) Tell your general that I want the barracks and all the supplies in the arsenal.
Narrator 2: The soldier returns to General Shepard and then returns to speak to Captain Shays.
Shays: What does your general have to

say now?
Soldier: I must warn you, Captain Shays, that General Shepard is prepared to order his troops to fire on you and your men.
Shays: That is what we want him to do.
Soldier: Do you have any message for General Shepard?
Shays: Tell him that I plan to take the arsenal on that hill.
Narrator 2: The soldier returns to his commander, and Captain Shays orders his men to march toward the arsenal. When the rebels are only one hundred yards from the militia, General Shepard orders his men to fire the cannon twice over Shays's men's heads. Shays commands his men to continue marching. Then the cannon fires directly into the farmers three times. The rebels yell out in surprise, break ranks, and run for their lives. Shays cannot reassemble them. The battle is over.

Three men—Ezckiel Root, Ariel Webster, and Jabez Spicer—are killed instantly. John Hunter is badly wounded and dies the following day. Shays collects his men about five miles east of Springfield and leads them to Ludlow, where they rest that night. He is nervous because General Benjamin Lincoln's troops are not far away and more that two hundred of his rebels have deserted.

Captain Shays and his depleted band continue to run from General Lincoln. They join Luke Day and his men in the loyal rebel town of Amherst the next morning. Nearly every man in the town leaves with Shays on January 28 for Pelham, where the farmers intend to defend themselves.

Act I, Scene 5

Narrator 1: Daniel Shays's farmhouse in

Pelham on January 29, 1787. Shays and the other rebel leaders are meeting when a messenger from General Lincoln appears.

Shays: I see that you carry a flag of truce. You must be from General Lincoln.

Messenger: Yes, sir. The general is in Hadley, and he sends you a message.

Shays: What does the general have to say to me?

Messenger: General Lincoln advises you to break up your band of farmers. If you agree to do this, General Lincoln promises to recommend to the General Court that the farmers be pardoned.

Shays: What about my staff and me? Will we be pardoned as well?

Messenger: The general did not mention anything about pardoning you or your officers.

Shays: Let me confer with my staff for a few minutes, and I will have a reply for you to take back to General Lincoln.

Narrator 2: The messenger leaves the farmhouse, and Shays talks to his officers.

Shays: What do you think of this offer?

William Conkey: What choice do we have? We are outnumbered and cannot expect many more reinforcements. Lincoln surely can get more troops, guns, and ammunition.

Luke Day: It will only be a matter of time before we are all killed or put into jail.

Shays: We must ask that everyone, including the officers, be pardoned.

Day: And Lincoln must take his militia back to Boston.

Conkey: The General Court should be urged to act on the petitions we sent to them.

Shays: That is a great deal to expect, but we have to give it a try. We all fought together to win our freedom from the British.

"Enough blood has been shed between brothers. It is time for peace and reconciliation."

Enough blood has been shed between brothers. It is time for peace and reconciliation.

Narrator 1: Shays writes out their terms, and the messenger leaves the next morning to deliver it to General Lincoln. Lincoln immediately replies that he has no authority to grant a pardon to everyone.

Shays and his depleted force move on to Petersham, with Lincoln following close behind. It is there that the general catches up with the rebels and confronts them with muskets and cannon. When the farmers realize that they do not stand a chance against the cannon, they disband and run out of town.

The Massachusetts militia catches one hundred fifty of the rebels. Since most of them are not officers, they are pardoned and are required only to swear an oath of allegiance to the Massachusetts government before they are allowed to go home. But the government puts a price on the heads of Shays and some of his officers, including Luke Day. They and several rebels continue to travel around New England stirring up trouble and even recruit some more men to their side. The last battle of Shays's Rebellion is fought near Sheffield on February 27, 1787. By September 1787, order is restored in western Massachusetts, and on June 13, 1788, even the leaders of the rebellion, including Shays, are pardoned.

Shays's Rebellion did not solve the problems of the farmers, but it certainly brought attention to the unjust laws and internal troubles that the young nation had to confront. Shays and his followers made their contribution to the growth of democracy, and we all have good reason to be thankful for their determination and courage.

Resource Activities

True or False?

1. Daniel Shays organized and led a group of farmers who opposed the debtor laws of the General Court.

2. Shays was a merchant who fought on behalf of farmers in debt.

3. The farmers of Pelham, Massachusetts, and the surrounding areas chose Shays as a leader because they were afraid to take on the responsibility themselves.

4. Shays and his men decided to use force instead of words to oppose the courts.

5. The purpose of the Riot Act passed by the General Court in Boston was to end all confrontations between angry farmers and the courts.

6. A right of habeas corpus protected citizens from being put in jail without just cause.

7. Governor Bowdoin of Massachusetts first ordered the courts to attempt to solve the debtor crisis. When this did not work, he advised passage of the Riot Act.

8. Shays was eager to engage the Massachusetts troops in a battle.

9. Shays's men fled as soon as Major General William Shepard ordered his men to fire the cannon.

10. General Benjamin Lincoln promised that if Shays disbanded his men, he would see to it that Shays and all his men were pardoned.

Do You Remember?

1. Why did the farmers choose to close the courts as their first goal?

2. Why did Daniel Shays sell the sword the Marquis de Lafayette gave him?

3. What were the provisions of the Riot Act?

4. What were some of the reasons the farmers gave Shays to convince him that he would be a good leader?

5. Was the Riot Act ever enforced during Shays's Rebellion?

6. What advice did Rufus Putnam give Shays?

7. What was the Worcester Petition?

8. What made Shays decide to lead his troops in rebellion against the courts?

9. Did the Massachusetts legislature act on the petitions sent by Shays and his fellow farmers?

10. Was Shays ever pardoned?

What Do You Think?

1. Why were the farmers in western Massachusetts so burdened with debt?

2. Why did the farmers band together, especially since their acts would be considered treasonous?

3. Why did the farmers want a leader who had no record of rebellious acts against the government? Would a leader experienced in rebellious acts have been better?

4. Why did Daniel Shays and the others not go to the General Court in Boston to present their case?

5. Why did Shays's friends disapprove of his selling the sword Lafayette gave him?

6. Why were the provisions of the Riot Act so harsh?

7. Why did the rebels submit the Worcester Petition?

8. What would have happened if General William Shepard had not ordered his men to fire at Shays and his men?

9. Why did Shays's men break ranks and flee so readily?

10. Why did the Massachusetts legislature and courts pardon the rebels?

From the Historical Perspective

1. Why was each state so insistent on its rights to make laws for its own citizens without interference from Congress?

2. After the Revolution, why did Britain forbid its colonies to trade with the United States? Why did Britain impose taxes and trade regulations on goods being imported and exported by the states?

3. Why did Shays's Rebellion make Americans more willing to accept a central government that had power over the states?

Further Activities

1. The land Ordinance of 1785 was successful. Research how this system of land division was designed to work. Research the rules Congress established in the Northwest Ordinance of 1787 to govern this land. On a map of the United States, shade in the area covered by the Northwest Territory and outline the five states that were carved out of it.

2. Every state in the United States still has the right to make laws governing its own citizens. As a result, laws and regulations differ from state to state. Make a list or a chart with the name of your state in one column and the name of a state that borders yours in another. Compare laws concerning personal state income tax, gun possession, safety belts, billboards, irradiation of produce, toxic waste cleanup, car insurance, and any other areas where you find the states differ in their rulings.

3. The laws of the United States are in a constant state of change. The courts are continually being asked to review decisions and to resolve new, untested situations. In Daniel Shays's day, there was no Supreme Court. Shays felt that there was no other way to resolve his problem except to forcibly stop the courts from meeting. If Shays lived today, how many courts could hear his case? Could he take his case to the Supreme Court in Washington, D.C.? What are the prerequisites to appear in each court?

TEACHER'S GUIDE

The plays in this book focus on events surrounding the American Revolution and the colonists' struggle for freedom. At the beginning of each chapter is a historical overview that provides background leading to the action in the play or plays in that chapter and a map pinpointing the places and historical events covered in the play or plays. The illustrations accompanying the plays serve as visual stimulation.

While the plays are presented chronologically, they do not have to be read in this order. If a specific topic, such as Indians, spies, women, or George Washington, is being covered in class, the play relating to this theme can be incorporated into the curriculum. Since plays by nature bring readers and listeners into a closer, more intimate relationship with the characters portrayed, it is important to help the students feel part of the action. In this way, they can better understand the reasons for the actions and the sequence of subsequent events.

Suggested uses for each play include the following: (1) a separate unit to complement the period or a parallel topic (past or present) being covered in the classroom; (2) supplementary material assigned as extra work or as reading inside or outside the classroom; and (3) a special day activity where students read different parts at their seats or perform the play before the rest of the class. The introduction and informational passages may be read by one or more narrators.

Each chapter focuses on one aspect of U.S. history. The historical themes emphasized in each chapter are listed below.

Colonists vs. Native Americans: The Indians' struggle against the colonists to retain their lands

Children of the Revolution: The successful attempts of young people to contribute to the colonists' victory in the Revolution

Women of the Revolution: The selfless contributions of women patriots during the Revolution

The Foreigners at Valley Forge: The invaluable assistance given the colonists by non-Americans during the Revolution

The Victorious March to Vincennes: The difficulties encountered by Americans fighting the Revolution along the frontier

Revolution at Sea: The daring exploits of patriots who brought the Revolution to Britain's shores

Slaves for Freedom: The heroic achievements of blacks during the Revolution

The Quest for National Unity: The debtor crisis caused by the Revolution

Each chapter also contains four sets of resource activities. These include **True or False?** statements, which test students' retention of the basic facts mentioned in the play; **Do You Remember?** questions, which test the students' ability to retain what has been read; **What Do You Think?** questions, which allow students to think more critically about what they have read; and **From the Historical Perspective** situations and questions, which invite students to give their opinions concerning problems and events that resulted from actions described in the plays.

At the end of each chapter is a set of **Further Activities.** Their purpose is to provide activities that tie the plays, their themes, and their arguments to the historical period in which they occurred. These activities also should help relate the regular classroom curriculum material to the plays. These activities allow students to pursue the themes touched on in the plays on a broader base.

The **Answers** section in this guide provides answers to all questions accompanying each chapter. Please note that the answers to **What Do You Think?** and **From the Historical Perspective** are brief. Teachers and students may wish to present additional comments or elaborate on the answers given.

Chapter One

True or False?

1. False. Pontiac was the chief of the Ottawa. He united the Ottawa and many other tribes and led them against the British.

2. False. Pontiac heard of the Delaware Prophet's message and went of his own accord to consult him.

3. True.

4. False. The Indians met near the Ecorse River in a treeless valley. Their security was very tight, and their meeting was kept a secret.

5. False. Pontiac told the Indians to return to their villages and prepare for war while he did the preliminary work.

6. True.

7. False. According to Pontiac's plan, he and about fifty warriors planned to seek entrance by asking permission to perform a ceremonial dance for the British within the fort.

8. False. Major Gladwin knew that Pontiac and his warriors were armed, but he allowed them to enter because he had his men and weaponry stationed around the fort.

9. True.

10. False. The Indians did attack the other British forts, capturing all of them except Fort Detroit.

Do You Remember?

1. The Delaware Prophet represented the Great Spirit here on earth. If the Prophet supported Pontiac's cause, the Indians would also because they looked to the Great Spirit for guidance.

2. The French were primarily fur trappers. They did not come in great numbers to settle the land. The British were settlers and colonists. This area was seen as a potentially prosperous colony.

3. The chiefs joined Pontiac when they realized that he had the support of the Great Spirit and the cooperation of the French.

4. The dance would promote calmness on the British side, while the noise and commotion it created would provide a perfect cover for Indian spies circulating through the British fort.

5. Pontiac told those Indians who lived far away to return to their villages and prepare their weapons for the upcoming battles.

6. Once they heard that Pontiac had destroyed Fort Detroit, the chiefs were to raise the battle cry among their respective tribes.

7. The British offered bread and tobacco to Pontiac and his warriors.

8. Pontiac planned to approach the fort in the chill of early morning so that he and his warriors could wear blankets and not be questioned. Their weapons would be hidden under the blankets.

9. No. Soon after Pontiac left Fort Detroit for the second time, Major Gladwin learned that Fort Sandusky had been destroyed by the Indians.

10. No. The siege was long, and the British sent reinforcements. The conspiracy failed when the Indians wanted to return to their homelands to hunt before winter set in.

What Do You Think?

1. Historians feel that Pontiac would not have succeeded, since the Indians placed a high value on the authority of the Great Spirit. The fact that the Delaware Prophet spoke for the Great Spirit convinced many chiefs that Pontiac's cause had divine approval.

2. The Prophet appeared as a plain, simple individual at one with nature and himself. He was not concerned with impressing anyone. He had few needs and spent much time thinking and listening to the Great Spirit's wishes. Pontiac, on the other hand, was a powerful chief who wore the trappings of his rank. These heightened his power and control in the eyes of the Indians.

3. By adopting the customs, the Indians made themselves more dependent on white people. For example, the Indians did not manufacture guns. But when guns became their means of hunting for food, their food supply became dependent on white people. Also, the Indians

lost their identity, independence, self-confidence, and sense of self-worth when they abandoned the ways of their ancestors.

4. The French were fur traders, not settlers like the British. Also, many British people were involved in land deals. New World real estate was very popular and provided a tremendous opportunity for the British to make money.

5. The British had forts and an arsenal of weapons. If they learned of an impending attack, they could supply themselves with food, water, and ammunition, send for reinforcements, close up the fort, and wait out a siege or use enough firepower to rout the enemy. In a surprise attack, the Indians had the advantage of cutting off all supplies and waiting for a surrender.

6. The first visit was necessary and not just to spy. It was meant to relax the British and make them feel that Pontiac and his men wished to befriend them. This feeling would help Pontiac when he entered the fort armed on the second visit.

7. Pontiac did not want the British to suspect his motives. He wanted all to appear normal and to keep the British at ease. By returning to their homelands, the tribes could attack the nearest British fort. Chaos among the British would result.

8. Perhaps Pontiac became more relaxed about the preparations because his plans had gone so well. He also might not have thought about a spy in the Indian camp.

9. Major Gladwin was extremely calm and pretended nothing was different. He restrained his men, even though they were prepared for an attack. He allowed Pontiac and his men to leave peacefully, even though he knew they were armed. He appeared ready to do his duty yet unwilling to shed any more blood than was necessary.

10. Perhaps these individuals felt that they had more to gain if they won British, rather than Indian, approval.

From the Historical Perspective

1. Direct communication is always more effective than that through an interpreter. A person who makes the effort to learn the other's language almost always has the advantage. He or she understands

immediately what the other person says. He or she also catches the intonation and emphasis placed on each word and phrase. In translation, phrases and feelings can lose some of their impact.

2. The British realized that the question of land ownership had to be handled carefully. They hoped to defuse the problem by legally keeping the Indians to the west and the colonists to the east of the line. But many colonists had already settled to the west of the line. As more colonists arrived, the urge to move to open land would increase. Also, land speculation was rampant. Since the colonists were beginning to resent British control, they saw the Proclamation Line of 1763 as a move by England to further legislate all actions of the colonists.

Chapter Two

True or False?

1. True.

2. False. Master Beman obtained only one bateau and one small boat. Time did not allow him to arrange for more boats from other towns.

3. False. He went across with the first group, and Benedict Arnold crossed with the second group.

4. True.

5. False. Because of their geographic position and the loss of many young men to the Continental Army, the island was practically defenseless. Therefore, the people tried to keep the island officially neutral, favoring neither side.

6. False. The sailors on the *Unicorn* searched Martha's Vineyard for a suitable mast.

7. True.

8. False. Peter was kidnapped as a young child and abandoned in the American Colonies.

9. False. Peter was eager to join the Continental Army and asked the judge for permission to enlist.

10. True.

Do You Remember?

1. Fort Ticonderoga was located at the southern end of Lake Champlain, on the border between New York and present-day Vermont.

2. Benedict Arnold held the rank of second in command during the capture of Fort Ticonderoga.

3. Nathan used to row across the lake to the fort. He loved to play spy, and the British never bothered or questioned him.

4. Captain Delaplace was the commander.

5. They tossed British tea into the hole dug for the Liberty Pole.

6. Maria Allen brought the auger, which was used to drill holes in the base of the Liberty Pole. Gunpowder was then put into the holes.

7. She had to have some means of igniting the gunpowder. Since coals were readily available in Colonial houses and would be easy to obtain, their heat would surely serve the purpose.

8. Peter's sister screamed and fought so fiercely that she managed to wriggle out of their arms and run back home.

9. Patrick Henry's powerful ending was "Give me liberty or give me death."

10. Washington advised that the Colonial soldiers wear something white, a visible mark in the dark.

What Do You Think?

1. The colonists did not manufacture these items. They were dependent on England for them. In a war, England definitely would not supply the opposition, even if the opposition were its subjects.

2. No one knows for sure, but children generally were not suspected of spying, especially in 1775, before the Revolutionary War spread throughout the Colonies. The British probably felt that their position was secure, with the lake protecting them from surprise attacks. The fort's location near Canada also made it less likely to be attacked.

3. Master Beman believed in the Revolutionary cause and, as a result, believed that a person must do what was in his or her power to help

further the cause of liberty. Master Beman most likely believed that the plan was well thought out and that the leader was confident and in command. The opportunity and potential for success were definitely there.

4. Postponement might have caused a cancellation. He also did not have approval from the Second Continental Congress. If the British learned of his plans, the element of surprise would be gone. From Nathan he had learned of a careless sentry and a weak point in the defenses. His men were dedicated and ready; they might hesitate if a postponement was ordered.

5. Most likely they feared retaliation against their island. Enough islanders were involved in the Continental Army to make their neutrality suspect. The girls did not want to jeopardize the lives and businesses of their families and fellow islanders.

6. Probably not. The British did not punish the islanders or exact payment because they realized that none of the selectmen knew the circumstances surrounding the blowup. Children were not considered suspects. If adults had been found to blame, the British would have exacted some retribution, and the island perhaps would have lost its neutral standing.

7. Yes. Geographically, Martha's Vineyard could have easily been overtaken by the British. This would have given the British a resupply point close to the Colonies, especially Massachusetts. By remaining neutral, islanders could still supply the mainland, allow smugglers and privateers to use its ports, and send men to join the Continental Army.

8. At five years old (or almost five as some sources believe), Peter was poised, dignified, and reserved. His polite manner and sense of self-assuredness showed good upbringing. Any person, especially a youngster, who had survived such an ordeal certainly had a strong character. Within a relatively short period, Peter also had learned enough English to converse fluently—a mark of determination. The youngster had accepted life's events and was ready and eager to go on.

9. The risk was high. In the battle, seventeen of the twenty advance men were killed. The reward needed to be high enough to spur the men on and make them forget the odds and their fears.

10. The attack was to be a surprise. Quiet was absolutely necessary. The sighting of an enemy, a nervous trigger finger, or an animal suddenly crossing the path could have caused a loaded musket to be fired, signaling their presence to the enemy. The trigger of an unloaded musket may have been pulled without such results. The bayonets provided a weapon and an extra sense of security for the Colonials.

From the Historical Perspective

1. Fort Ticonderoga controlled the principal route to and from Canada. The fort was on Lake Champlain, which connected the Hudson River flowing through New York with the St. Lawrence River flowing through Canada. Since Canada was controlled by the British, they could use this waterway to resupply and reinforce their troops. If the colonists had the fort, this passageway would be closed. In addition, colonists would have access to Canada and to neighboring French Canadians (after the French and Indian War) who might be enlisted to help.

2. In revolutionary times, people need rallying points to give them confidence, a sense of togetherness, and a feeling that they are not alone fighting the opposition. A particularly good rallying point is a visible one that causes no harm and offends no one but symbolizes the cause. The Liberty Pole is a good example. A support system is necessary if a revolution is to succeed. Committees and groups were an essential ingredient in the colonists' success.

3. The Colonials had fewer soldiers than the British. The Colonials were not as well trained; many had never fought before. Ammunition, cannon, and other weapons were in short supply in the Continental Army. To overcome these disadvantages, the colonists often resorted to night and surprise attacks.

Chapter Three

True or False?

1. False. The colonel was planning to sell the yearling. The Colonial army needed all the horses it could get.

2. False. She was worried about outlaws, Tories, and deserters on the night road, but she realized that Sybil was the only choice.

3. False. She rode the yearling only to do errands. Sybil loved horses, but she had no plan other than convincing her father to keep the yearling.

4. True.

5. True.

6. False. Lydia objected because she did not want the British to take over her house. Much of Lydia's information came as a result of her house's close proximity to the British headquarters in Philadelphia.

7. False. Lydia never told her husband the real reason for her walk. She felt that his answers and reactions to any British questioning would be more credible if he did not know her reasons.

8. False. The British suspected the Zane family but never learned the identity of the horse thief.

9. False. Several of Colonel Zane's men also volunteered, but Betty's argument that a woman would be less suspect than a man made her the choice.

10. True.

Do You Remember?

1. The other men were allowed to return home to begin spring plowing and planting.

2. Colonel Ludington had to remain at his farm and wait for the arrival of the militiamen, then brief them and organize them into fighting units.

3. The British had attacked and burned under-protected Danbury. They would continue to destroy other underprotected towns unless the Colonial militiamen could warn the townspeople ahead of the British troops' arrival. The sooner Colonel Ludington left, the better were his chances of saving another

town from destruction.

4. Sybil did not want to take any chances. If British soldiers or spies reported her actions, her ride would be in vain. If highwaymen captured her, she could not warn the other militiamen.

5. Lydia told her husband of her observations and news of the British. He wrote them in shorthand. She then placed the paper on a button, covered it with cloth, and sewed the button back onto its proper garment. When her younger son, the wearer of the garment, arrived at the Colonial camp, Lydia's older son took off the button, took out the paper, recovered the button, and sewed it back onto the garment.

6. Lydia was a Quaker, and Quakers are known pacifists. The Darraghs, especially Lydia, also were on friendly terms with the British. She had always cooperated with their requests. Lydia had never given them any reason to doubt her motives.

7. Lydia knew the message had to get through to General Washington. She could not make it to his camp in time and feared that if she told only one person and that person did not make it, Washington and Whitemarsh would be unprepared for the attack. By telling two people, she felt sure that at least one would get through.

8. She tied the reins of each horse to the pommel of the preceding horse. In this way, she could guide the lead horse, and the others would follow along.

9. The women cleaned, cooled, and loaded the rifles. They also stored the food supplies.

10. Betty reasoned that the British and the Indians would be startled to see a young woman running out from the fort. Because of this, it would take a while for them to react.

What Do You Think?

1. The courier was so exhausted that he might have collapsed, fallen from his horse, and injured himself and the horse. Furthermore, his exhaustion might have prevented him from being as careful as he might otherwise have been. He also could have been caught by Tories or seen by spies, both of whom would alert the British. Colonel Ludington

would not know of any of this until it was too late for his militiamen to react and be effective.

2. The times were frightening. Spies and false rumors were everywhere. It was not always easy to get the truth. The colonists learned to be careful and wary of whatever they saw and heard.

3. The thirteen colonies did not have ready supplies of ammunition. When the Revolutionary War broke out, the British controlled the ammunition and weapons, and the colonists were forced to use their personal weapons or those they managed to obtain by various other means.

4. The militiamen were truly committed to the Colonial cause. They wasted no time in rousing themselves from their beds, preparing their horses, and assembling immediately at Colonel Ludington's farm. The spirit and courage of the militiamen made them ready to act at a moment's notice.

5. Lydia could use visits to her children, especially the younger children, as her reason for being in places where she otherwise should not have been. It allowed her more freedom and better opportunities to carry out her espionage.

6. Yes. With the British using the Darragh house, the family was suspect. A person who knows something and tries to feign ignorance is much more likely to be detected than one who knows nothing. Lydia knew this and acted accordingly. She also knew that her family would be worried the whole time she was gone. Their anxiety could easily give them away.

7. Lydia did not know how events would turn out. Even if the maid were completely trustworthy, Lydia's plans might have had to change suddenly, and escaping a dangerous situation is more difficult for two than it is for one. Also, if the mission was successful, the Darraghs would be questioned. If no one in the household knew anything, then Lydia's story would seem much more credible.

8. In 1782, many men were off fighting in the Revolutionary War. Others were off on business or out trapping and hunting. Forts offered safety during attacks and raids, expecially to women and children who often were alone in frontier cabins.

9. If no new supply of gunpowder could be secured, defeat was inevitable and Simon Girty and his party would surely overrun the fort, showing mercy to no one. Fetching the gunpowder would give Colonel Zane and his men the chance to succeed. Betty successfully argued that every man was needed to cover the volunteer who would run to the cabin. Fear of what might occur without the gunpowder made the colonel willing to try anything.

10. Simon Girty realized that Colonel Zane's men—with their new supply of gunpowder—could defend the fort and gradually kill off his men one by one. Since his force was small, about three hundred fifty men, Girty would soon lose much of his fighting power.

From the Historical Perspective

1. The British soldiers were part of a trained army. The colonists were not trained soldiers. They were skilled in protecting themselves, not in fighting major battles. The colonists also needed to tend to their daily chores to keep their families fed, clothed, and housed. Few could afford to spend much time away from home. The Colonial army also had few provisions and little equipment.

2. In 1764, the British Parliament passed the Quartering Act, which required American colonists to house and feed British troops. While this practice was commonly accepted as a duty in England, it was not accepted by many in the Colonies. In 1774, the Quartering Act was renewed under the British Parliament's passage of the Coercive Acts. Furthermore, General Howe had captured Philadelphia and felt the city was totally under British control.

3. The American colonists had four basic advantages: They knew the terrain better than the British; they were better marksmen than the British; their guns had a longer firing range; and they had a definite self-motivating factor—freedom and independence.

Chapter Four

True or False?

1. False. His troops built log huts and earthworks as a defense system when they arrived in December.

2. False. Washington met Lafayette earlier, in July 1777. Washington had heard about him from Benjamin Franklin and was greatly impressed by him.

3. True.

4. False. Washington felt that such appointments would be unfair, especially since his soldiers had learned and endured so much on the battlefield.

5. False. Von Steuben had heard of the American Revolution from Benjamin Franklin in Paris. American agents there asked him to travel to America to train the Continental Army.

6. True.

7. False. Von Steuben picked a company of men and trained them. He then sent them back to their units with a drillmaster so that they could teach the drill routine to their fellow soldiers. Von Steuben then chose another company of men and proceeded the same way.

8. False. Von Steuben liked the challenge, and he stayed and drilled the troops, shaping them into a trained military organization.

Do You Remember?

1. No command was given. The appointment was an honorary title.

2. Lafayette planned to name his son George Washington Lafayette as a tribute to his hero. (N.B. Lafayette did follow through on this promise.)

3. Lafayette, like Washington, accepted no pay. Lafayette was committed to the cause of freedom and volunteered his services.

4. Yes. In September 1777, he fought at Brandywine, where he was wounded. In November 1777, he fought at Gloucester. The courage and skill he displayed were contributing factors to Washington's recommendation that he be appointed commander of a division.

5. Benjamin Franklin, the head American agent in Paris, wrote General Washington about von Steuben's capabilities.

6. Von Steuben was quite shocked and surprised at their attitude and lack of training. He compared them to a herd of cows.

7. Von Steuben had trained, fought, and seen many different armies and strategies in Europe. He also knew that the British were as well trained as any troops. To defeat them would require an army trained in discipline and military strategy.

8. Von Steuben was amazed at the soldiers' independent spirit. They did not take orders as his European troops had; they questioned him as to why such a drill or technique was necessary.

What Do You Think?

1. The monarchy ruled France in 1777. If the United States was to receive aid, it had to be approved by the king. The marquis came from a well-respected family. His wife was the daughter of a duke who also was of social importance. The king depended on his nobles for their support in wars and other crises. He could not afford to slight them. Therefore, the marquis would have had easy access to the monarch, and his pleas and requests would have received careful attention.

2. Lafayette considered Washington a gentleman like himself. He saw him as a man thoroughly committed to a righteous cause, a man who asked no pay for his services but served tirelessly because of his beliefs, a man concerned with the welfare of his fellow citizens, and a man willing to sacrifice his life for his beliefs. Lafayette admired those qualities and sought to possess them.

3. Such decisions were probably very difficult for Washington, since he knew the colonists had to win battles to win the war. But he also knew that appointing foreigners over Americans would hurt the morale of his men. This would spread discontent and cause desertion among the troops. Washington had to tread very carefully and appraise the whole picture in addition to each situation.

4. Washington admired Lafayette's courage and bravery as well as his willingness to fight for what he believed was a just cause. Washington also must have admired Lafayette's determination. Lafayette had hoped for a commission immediately. When he did not receive it, he still fought bravely. He wanted his country to support Washington and the Revolutionary cause, yet he did not get discouraged and give up when his efforts seemed of little use at first. He persisted until the king finally approved support for the Americans.

5. Von Steuben's training gave the Americans the confidence they needed to believe that they could defeat the British. The discipline also made them see themselves as a fighting unit, each person responsible for a particular action and duty. Von Steuben's training gave them a sense of belonging, a camaraderie among the troops that helped drive away the loneliness and depression.

6. Von Steuben was a direct, forceful man. He was honest and explained to the men the necessity of drilling. His goal was a well-trained army capable of defeating the British. The soldiers recognized this and agreed with his aims. In addition to the military reasons for the drills, they took the soldiers' minds off the wretched conditions at Valley Forge.

7. The soldiers were colonists, not professional military personnel. They had enlisted to fight for freedom, not to be ordered about, especially by an unknown foreigner who happened to offer his services to their general. The patriots seeking freedom had thought about their rights and the justness of the cause they were serving. As a result, they questioned everything, especially since they could be imprisoned or even tried for treason if the Americans lost the war or were captured.

8. Von Steuben was a rugged individual who did not demand or expect comforts at Valley Forge. He accepted the cold and scarcities as part of the struggle in which he and the colonists were involved. He did not let his lack of knowledge of English deter him from his purpose. He wisely requested an aide who knew American customs. He did not ridicule or refuse to tolerate American customs. He carefully planned his strategy, disciplining one group at a time and then sending them back as teachers. He did not let

the lack of so many essentials and necessities at Valley Forge destroy his purpose. He had his goal, and he pursued it.

From the Historical Perspective

1. France was a major European power. It had a trained army and, more importantly, a trained navy, which the United States especially lacked. Since France had fought England in many wars, its military and its people would be more willing to support a confrontation that would result in the defeat of an enemy. France also could provide urgently needed military supplies and funds in addition to manpower.

2. British general Howe and his troops had ravaged the countryside on their way to Philadelphia. In fact, both British and American troops tried to eliminate each other's food supplies in an attempt to weaken the enemy. In addition, Congress had little money and argued over how to spend it. Consequently, little filtered through to the army.

Chapter Five

True or False?

1. True.

2. False. Henry warned Clark that he would have difficulty, especially if the great dangers involved in the march were known.

3. False. Henry planned to tell only the leaders of Virginia's executive council. There was no time to do anything else. Henry also did not feel it wise to inform too many people. Secrecy and surprise were the keys to success.

4. True.

5. False. He gave orders to his leaders to warn the soldiers not to be destructive, cruel, or belligerent once they captured Kaskaskia. Clark realized that in order to capture Cahokia and Detroit, he needed the Kaskaskians as allies.

6. False. Clark managed to capture both Vincennes and Cahokia without firing a shot.

7. False. Under Clark's orders, Fort Sackville at

Vincennes was flying the American flag. The commander, Captain Leonard Helm, had been sent to Vincennes by Clark. Clark, however, was not at the fort. Hamilton knew this, but he realized the importance of Vincennes and was determined to keep the British flag flying over it.

8. True.

9. False. Willie Chalmers was orphaned at Cahokia. All of his family had been killed by hostile Indians. Clark felt sorry for Willie and invited him to come along despite his reservations about the dangers of the mission.

10. False. Clark sent a scout to look for the supply boat but found no sign of it. Clark could not wait any longer and continued his march to Vincennes without the supplies.

Do You Remember?

1. Clark argued that the frontier protected the settled lands and that if the executive council did not feel that the frontier was worth protecting, then the council should not claim it. Clark added that some other country, especially England, might consider the frontier more valuable than the executive council.

2. His nickname was "Hair-Buyer" Hamilton. It was given to him because Hamilton supposedly paid Indians to bring him American scalps.

3. Clark felt that a band of 500 men would be sufficient, but he recruited only 275.

4. Clark did not want the British to know that his troops were about. In the wilderness, noise travels and the British might hear the shots. Since different guns make different sounds, an unfamiliar gunshot would cause a British sentry or sympathizer to investigate and sound an alarm.

5. Wild blackberries, dewberries, and raspberries were in season. The men could pick them at will.

6. Detroit was Clark's goal, but it was the British headquarters and was heavily garrisoned and armed. Since Clark had a small army, he knew he had to rely on strategy, courage, and resourcefulness. If his troops were better trained and supplies were increased, his

chances of victory would be greater. Therefore, Clark opted to train his troops further and resupply before marching on Detroit.

7. Father Gibault appreciated the lack of bloodshed. He commended Clark for taking Cahokia and Vincennes without firing a shot.

8. A Spanish merchant named Francis Vigo informed Clark about Hamilton's recapture of Vincennes.

9. Clark's forces numbered about 275 men. He knew they would be defeated if Hamilton's far greater numbers were prepared. Clark felt he could win only if he attacked by surprise and took control of Fort Sackville and Vincennes before Hamilton could organize and ready his men for a fight.

10. The area near Vincennes was flat prairie. Water from rain and snow does not run off this type of land, as there are no hills or sloping areas. Also, the earth is so tightly packed that the soil is not porous and does not absorb the water.

What Do You Think?

1. Patrick Henry admired Clark's sincerity, enthusiasm, and willingness to undertake projects. When Clark proposed a strategy or goal, Henry knew that he had carefully thought out the advantages, disadvantages, benefits, and risks involved. Henry also recognized in Clark the courage and fortitude to pursue and fight for a goal in which he believed.

2. Clark and his men were marching through Indian and enemy territory. Any attack on them could mean annihilation. The whole plan would be defeated, since Clark had no backup troops or reinforcements. If his men thought they were lost, they might panic.

3. Yes. If a parcel of land is claimed by a nation and another nation decides to claim it, the first nation must take verbal, legal, or military action to maintain control over the land. If the first nation opts to do nothing, the second nation will easily control the land.

4. Clark had few men, many of whom were new recruits. Every man counted, as did every bullet and piece of food. He could not afford to make mistakes. If one of his men was given an order, he had to do it.

Forgetting or losing one's bearings was no excuse. It could cause the annihilation of the entire force. Clark had to convey this to Saunders. A death threat definitely conveyed the gravity of the situation and also set an example.

5. Even after the British defeated the French in the French and Indian War, there were many French frontiersmen and settlers west of the Alleghenies. Many of these French were Catholic. French missionaries had traveled west of the Alleghenies seeking converts and exploring new lands. The French priests were highly regarded and their advice heeded. If Father Gibault favored Clark, other Frenchmen would follow.

6. Captain Helm realized that his troops were greatly outnumbered by the British. Engaging in battle meant almost certain annihilation. If he did not surrender, Fort Sackville would definitely suffer in the battle and thwart Clark's plans to use recruits from Vincennes to aid in the capture of Detroit. Helm also knew that Clark was nearby and possibly could defeat Hamilton. Given the circumstances, the advantages of facing certain defeat did not outweigh the advantages of surrender.

7. Vigo had promised Colonel Hamilton that he would go to St. Louis. Since Hamilton did not want Clark to know he had retaken Fort Sackville, Vigo might have thought that Hamilton ordered someone to follow him. Once he arrived in St. Louis, it was safe for Vigo to tell Clark that the British had control of Fort Sackville and Vincennes.

8. The *Willing* had Clark's ammunition and artillery supplies. If these supplies were captured, it would be a great loss to the Americans. Since informants were everywhere, Captain Rogers had to make sure no one learned of his presence or his plans. Secrecy and surprise were needed for the Americans to succeed. Hostile Indian parties also roamed the frontier, seeking to drive out settlers. Captain Rogers's ship and supplies, both military and domestic, would be put to immediate use by almost anyone who could defeat his small contingent.

9. Supplies and morale were low; living conditions were wretched. Clark decided that if he banned hunting, his men might lose the will to keep going. Clark decided it was worth the risk. Fresh meat would certainly give his army more strength and also would improve morale.

10. Clark realized that his men had to have something else to think of besides the wretched march. Diversions such as singing, preparing the night's meal, and competition among companies to serve the most creative meal all improved morale. However, if he did not participate, the men might have felt that he was patronizing them and above such behavior. By joining in, he became their equal for that moment. Consequently, he won even more respect.

From the Historical Perspective

1. According to the Treaty of Paris, which was signed in 1763 by Britain and France after the French and Indian War, Spain had the right to claim New Orleans and the lands west of the Mississippi River. This tremendous expanse of land was known as the Louisiana Territory. Consequently, Spain controlled the Mississippi River and the port of New Orleans. Spain also claimed Florida. Spanish traders and merchants were engaged in exporting goods such as produce, silver, gold, and furs from the New World.

2. The British claimed not only the thirteen colonies but also the lands to the west as far as the Mississippi River, except for New Orleans and Florida. Since Britain also claimed Canada, its troops could land, headquarter, and supply or resupply themselves in Canada and march south along the western boundaries of the thirteen colonies. The British also could join forces with Indian tribes. Such moves could squeeze the colonists from both the West and the East. The colonists had to watch both sides.

3. There are many possible reasons. The great battles in the East centered on major cities. George Washington and other Revolutionary leaders were more closely involved in these battles, as were the major British generals. The majority of Americans also lived in the East. The Declaration of Independence, the Continental Congress, and the articles and news clippings being circulated all originated in the East.

Chapter Six

True or False?

1. False. Jones did assume command of the *Ranger* and captured an English naval vessel with it. He sent it back to America because it was slow and he hoped for the command of a stronger, faster warship.

2. False. Jones hoped his friends at the French court would be able to get the king to give him a warship. When this did not happen, Jones went to see the king himself. Louis XVI gave Jones an old French merchant ship that he converted into a warship.

3. False. Jones had to recruit whatever sailors he could. Few American sailors were in France. Jones did recruit some Americans, but many were British deserters.

4. True. Jones named the ship after Franklin's *Poor Richard's Almanac*.

5. False. Jones was given command of the *Bon Homme Richard* and several other ships—the American-built *Alliance* and three French-built vessels, the *Pallas*, the *Cerf*, and the *Vengeance*.

6. False. Jones planned to take some high-ranking citizens of Leith as prisoners and to destroy as many ships as possible in its harbor before making a quick exit.

7. False. Jones wrote the letter, but he gave it to Lieutenant Colonel de Chamillard to deliver to the mayor.

8. False. Several cannon did burst, but the men on the *Bon Homme Richard* refused to try the other eighteen-pounders for fear they also would burst.

9. True.

10. False. In the midst of the battle, the *Alliance* shot at the *Bon Homme Richard* several times before sailing off.

Do You Remember?

1. Franklin advised Jones that if a person wanted to have business negotiations done well, that person should do them himself. If the person did not care, then he could ask another person to do them for him.

2. The French privateers *Monsieur* and *Granville* quit the squadron after a disagreement. The *Cerf* got caught in a storm and returned to France. The *Alliance* moved independently of Jones's fleet and was unreliable.

3. Jones lowered a small boat and sent it with a crew to check out Leith's ships and to find out how many of them had guns.

4. Captain Pearson immediately ordered the British merchant ships he was escorting to seek safety in the nearest British port. He and the smaller British warship, the *Countess of Scarborough*, began to sail toward the *Bon Homme Richard*.

5. The wind. At Leith, a sudden gale began to blow offshore and prevented Jones from entering the harbor. Later, a wind blew hard enough to send the *Bon Homme Richard* within firing range of the *Serapis*. Then a light breeze made the ships float together so that Jones could steer the *Bon Homme Richard* within boarding range of the *Serapis*.

6. Several of the old eighteen-pound guns exploded during their first discharge, killing and wounding many of Jones's men. As a result, Jones's crew was very dejected. They refused to fire the other eighteen-pounders. It was Jones's enthusiasm and personal support as he walked around the lower decks encouraging the men that gave the crew courage to fight.

7. The cannon fire from the *Serapis* was tearing the old, rotten timbers of the *Bon Homme Richard*, while the new timbers of the *Serapis* were hardly affected by the cannon fire of the American vessel. Jones knew that his ship would be demolished or would sink if he remained within firing range of the *Serapis*. His alternatives were to retreat out of range or to bring the *Bon Homme Richard* up close to the *Serapis* and board the ship.

8. Jones replied, "I have not yet begun to fight."

9. The *Bon Homme Richard* caught on fire, as had the *Serapis*. If the fire reached the storeroom where the gunpowder was kept, the heat from the fire would cause the gunpowder to explode. Such an explosion would mean certain defeat and probably death. The ship could not survive such an explosion.

10. Jones had positioned sharpshooters on the *Bon Homme Richard* and had ordered them to fire at the *Serapis*'s crew. He also had ordered sailors into the rigging to throw hand

grenades into the open areas of the *Serapis*. Pearson saw his ship ablaze and decided to surrender, thereby sparing as many lives as possible.

What Do You Think?

1. Later events proved that it was a wise decision. It left him free to take command of the *Duc de Duras*. The decision also proved that Jones was a man with a definite goal and a firm sense of what was needed to accomplish that goal. Jones knew he needed a ship fast enough to outmaneuver those he would be chasing and large enough to hold the cannon he felt were necessary to capture the ships he chased. Without these prerequisites, he believed it made no sense to try to pursue his goal. Defeat, loss of a slow ship, and loss of lives would certainly follow, and not one of these would give anyone cause to grant him a better ship. It was better to wait.

2. The *Duc de Duras* had great potential. The ship was big and could hold many cannon. These were two of Jones's most important prerequisites. Since time was passing, Jones could not keep waiting. He believed that with proper reconditioning, the *Duc de Duras* would prove itself a worthy warship. Jones also would have the opportunity to make his own modifications to the ship and to rearrange and recondition it as he saw fit.

3. We do not know the answer, but replacing the cannon cost money, and funds were limited. If he tested one and it burst, his officers and crew might feel that all the equipment was too old and that the ship might be unseaworthy in a heavy battle. They might refuse to sail with him, and recruiting sailors at this time was very difficult. If he did not test the cannon and acted confidently about the *Duc de Duras*, this air of confidence would pass to his men. The eighteen-pounders were huge guns, and just their presence on the deck would give the crew a sense of protection and invulnerability. They would cause an enemy ship to respect the *Duc de Duras*'s potential and its awesome appearance.

4. Jones had no say in the matter. Although he was commander of his ship and the commander in chief of the squadron, Congress and circumstances determined which ships were in the squadron. Also, Jones's objections to any orders or personnel would take too much valuable time. Jones did not want to use any more time than was absolutely necessary.

5. Jones wanted to prove the might of the American Navy and show England it did not control the seas, not even its own coastline. A port town, especially a prosperous one, was ideal, since Jones intended to destroy all the merchant ships lying at anchor in the harbor. Such an act would make the English think twice about opposing the Revolution and feeling invincible on the seas. In addition, destroyed merchant ships would hurt the English economy and greatly anger English merchants. An attack on a port town would allow Jones to escape easily by sea. He did not plan to harm the citizens, for he knew this would hurt his plan and make the English angry with him and, in turn, with all Americans.

6. Merchant ships were defenseless. Their defeat did not prove his skill as a captain and naval officer. To attack only merchant ships would give him the reputation as a coward, fearful of actually doing battle with a warship. To prey on towns along the coast would do the same. The people were civilians, and terrorizing them was a bully's act. Jones wanted to prove his worth as a commander of a warship. He wanted to defeat a big English warship. A victory would greatly aid the American cause and would result in great concern and debate in Parliament and among loyal British subjects.

7. Jones was a determined, forceful man who was not easily deterred from his goal. He was not about to let the destruction of several guns at the outset of a great battle ruin or hurt his chances for victory. He knew that the men, not the guns, were now the problem. He knew that they needed encouragement, and he provided them with that immediately. He did not force them to try the other eighteen-pounders. This could bring on a mutiny or, at least, an argument. Jones wanted a victory badly. He cheered his men on, accenting the positive points of their ship and what they still had in the way of cannon and ammunition.

8. Pearson wanted to know if Jones had surrendered or was about to surrender.

When a captain struck his colors, he lowered his country's flag, which signaled surrender.

9. Jones never trusted Landais and did not have the time or the ammunition to fire back. He had his men signal to Landais and continued the battle for the *Serapis*. Jones was too busy overseeing raging fires, gaping holes with seawater pouring in, and dying men as the fierce battle between the *Bon Homme Richard* and the *Serapis* continued. The *Bon Homme Richard* as a ship was a wreck, and Landais's cannon fire did not make that much difference. Jones knew he had to board and capture the *Serapis* to claim victory.

10. Jones and his crew tried to save the ship, but they were unable to do so. Jones could not leave the ship floating about—such a vessel would become a navigational hazard, especially at night. The standard practice in a situation such as this is to sink the ship.

From the Historical Perspective

1. British merchants were prowar. They did not want to lose the lucrative trade with the Colonies. British land developers also were prowar, since they were greatly interested in land development and real estate sales. If the Colonies became independent, the British would no longer control the situation and British laws would no longer govern trade and land claims. When Jones began destroying British trading vessels, English merchants began to rethink the war policy. A vessel was a costly proposition, and fear of destruction at every crossing put too much pressure on the merchant ship crews and their owners, especially as the profits continued to decrease. So as not to lose everything, British merchants gradually pushed for the war to end. This affected Parliament's and the king's positions, since they depended on the merchant class for support and a solvent government.

2. Creating a navy is not simple. Few of the colonists were seamen. Few knew much about maneuvering large vessels. There was no time to practice or train. In addition, Congress had little money to build warships. The Continental Army, while not well trained or efficient in the beginning, had the advantages of knowing the terrain and could easily engage in guerrilla warfare. In addition, many colonists were great sharpshooters. These advantages added to the rebels' desire to win freedom and quickly made the Continental Army into a fairly efficient fighting force.

3. Although the Americans were inexperienced at fighting, regular soldiers and sailors could recognize a leader who was confident and knew what he was doing. They would trust him, obey him, and follow him. An inexperienced leader would have far more difficulty controlling his troops, especially in a desperate situation. Congress and the leaders of the colonists wanted to win. They had to make careful decisions. But Congress also had to be political. France was supplying troops, funds, and ships to the rebels. Some of these Frenchmen were already officers in their army and navy. Neglecting to give them command would have been an insult to France, which might have withdrawn its support to the Colonies. Since Congress realized that the Colonies could never hope to win without allies, foreign officers had to be included and treated fairly, if not favored. But Congress also had to be careful not to upset the soldiers and their leaders. Anger would cause resentment and mistrust.

Chapter Seven

True or False?

1. False. Phillis was born in Africa, captured, and brought across the Atlantic Ocean to the Colonies to be sold as a slave. The Wheatleys were her first and only owners.

2. False. All three members of the Wheatley family appreciated Phillis's alertness and encouraged her to study and learn all she could.

3. True.

4. False. Phillis's poems were well received even when she was a teen-ager. Her fame spread in the Colonies and in Europe, especially England. Her viewpoint as a black made her poems much more significant, especially since the issue of slavery was being discussed by people on both sides of the Atlantic.

5. False. Washington did not accompany

Lafayette. Washington sent Lafayette south to learn what he could about the British.

6. False. The Virginians refused to do either. They hid their horses and refused to accept American paper money in exchange for supplies.

7. True.

8. False. Lafayette welcomed Armistead's support and willingness to serve, but he made it clear to Armistead that he could not promise the slave his freedom.

9. False. Lafayette told Armistead to offer his services to General Benedict Arnold in his headquarters.

10. False. Armistead and his assistants managed to report any news to Lafayette within a couple of hours.

Do You Remember?

1. Susannah wanted someone young enough to care for her as she grew older. Many of her slaves were getting old, and she needed someone younger to take their place doing chores.

2. Mary, the daughter, was in charge of broadening Phillis's studies. Mary also had friends who helped educate Phillis.

3. John offered to submit Phillis's poems to his friend Archibald Bell, a London bookseller. He thought that because British presses were larger than American ones and were not affected by the Revolution, her poems would have a greater reception and would be more widely circulated.

4. The countess was a friend of the earl of Dartmouth, who was a friend of Reverend Whitefield, an ardent opponent of slavery. Phillis had dedicated a poem to the reverend. Phillis had heard of the countess from Reverend Whitefield and knew that she too was against slavery. Phillis admired the countess and probably believed that she could help abolish slavery.

5. Benedict Arnold, the American traitor, and Lord Charles Cornwallis.

6. Washington advised Lafayette to use spies and to learn as much as possible about the British troops' movement. Washington advised Lafayette not to attack the British because they were too strong for his small army.

7. Washington suggested that Lafayette recruit black troops. Armistead, a black slave, wanted to enlist in the Continental Army. After obtaining his master's permission, Armistead offered his services to Lafayette because he had heard that Lafayette needed recruits badly.

8. Armistead originally served General Benedict Arnold. After Arnold left for the North, he was transferred to Cornwallis's headquarters.

9. Armistead found it quite simple to gather information while he worked in Arnold's headquarters. Cornwallis, however, was a far more cautious man. He was very careful with his notes, maps, and any other information that might give the Americans an advantage.

10. Armistead petitioned the General Assembly of Virginia for his freedom. The Assembly paid Armistead's master a fair price for the slave's freedom.

What Do You Think?

1. The Wheatleys' position on slavery probably changed during the years Phillis lived with them. The Wheatleys had other slaves who performed the majority of the household chores. They might not have given much thought to the issue of slavery, but most likely they never mistreated their slaves. As Phillis grew and matured, the Wheatleys probably became more aware of slaves as people, rather than possessions, and began to consider the "right and wrong" of slavery. Although it is a matter of conjecture, it can be assumed that the Wheatleys began to oppose slavery or at least to push for the rights of slaves, since John Wheatley was willing to have Phillis's poems published.

2. Each individual can experience only so much. Reading helps a person understand what he or she cannot experience. In order to express one's feelings for a variety of people, a writer must understand his or her own situation and the situations and lifestyles of others. Reading helps a writer broaden his or her vocabulary, manner of expression, outlook on the world (past, present, and future), and comprehension of events.

3. America was in the midst of a revolution.

Materials were expensive and difficult to obtain in the New World. The issue of slavery was a sensitive one. Colonists took opposing views, and Phillis's poetry might have riled up more animosity at a time when conditions were difficult enough. England was a logical choice. It was far enough away from the arena of war, yet because of the circumstances, it was foremost in everyone's mind.

4. Yes. Her presence made the meaning and the message of her poems much more real. By being there, she probably won more supporters to her cause. Phillis also had the chance to explain her feelings and to counteract negative statements. Support from respected English citizens certainly enhanced her position.

5. The British hoped to make life so difficult for the Americans that they would stop fighting and surrender. Without horses, they could not travel, plow the fields, or train cavalry units. Without ammunition, they could not hunt or resist the British. Without food, the revolutionaries would cease to exist.

6. People hesitated to accept American paper money and considered it worthless because the government was new and did not have the resources to insure and secure its own currency. In addition, if the colonists lost their fight for freedom, the money printed by the American government would have no value, since the Colonies would still belong to England and be required to use British currency.

7. Washington did not have as many soldiers as the British. He could not afford to take risks. Supplies were crucial, and Lafayette's force was too small. Even if Lafayette managed to do some damage to Cornwallis, he most likely would lose men and ammunition. Keeping track of Cornwallis's moves was essential. Washington hoped to get Cornwallis in a position where the Continental Army would have a decisive advantage. This type of major victory was necessary to win the war.

8. Arnold had fought on the American side. He knew that the slaves generally preferred British rule. He also knew that they wanted to be free and that many believed freedom would be more easily obtained under the British. Therefore, it was only natural that the British would accept Armistead's story.

9. Cornwallis knew that there were many spies about. He used spies and had received much information in that way. He knew how clever spies could be. He also knew that no strategy would work well if the enemy learned of it beforehand. Cornwallis was a good general and determined to defeat the rebels. He purposely guarded all pertinent information, making it much more difficult for the enemy to surprise or outwit him.

10. Cornwallis realized that he was surrounded by American and French troops. He knew that the French fleet would prevent any help from arriving by sea. The American land forces also were not about to let reinforcements cross their lines. Cornwallis did hold out against cannon bombardment for ten days, but he did not want to incur any more casualties. When he realized that General Washington had an advantage, he surrendered to prevent further bloodshed, sorrow, and turmoil.

From the Historical Perspective

1. Many colonists, including Abigail Adams (John Adams's wife), believed that owning slaves was hypocritical. How could Americans fight for freedom for themselves and their families and at the same time refuse to grant freedom to others? In the North, slaves were usually found within the household doing chores. In the South, great numbers of slaves were used in the fields. In fact, plantation owners would not have survived and been able to produce such large quantities of marketable goods without the slaves. Many southerners felt that slavery was an economic necessity and could not see the inequity and injustice in the system.

2. Many people opposed black revolutionaries. They feared arming black slaves because they thought the slaves might run away, revolt, or otherwise fail to support the rebels' cause once they were free of the plantation or the slave owner's property and jurisdiction. The British offered freedom to slaves who joined their ranks. Many slaves opted to take advantage of the British offer. The colonists were aware of this and soon began to open their ranks to blacks. When blacks first joined Colonial units, they were not allowed to bear arms. Later, this policy was changed.

3. Benedict Arnold led the colonists against the British in many battles. He was an energetic leader who charged with his troops. He boldly faced the enemy on the battlefield and hardships on the trail. The colonists and the rebel leaders trusted him. When Major André was stopped with the information about Benedict Arnold's plans to turn West Point over to the British, the colonists were shocked. Major André was a sad case of someone duped by a master of evil. Arnold was cursed, rejected, and forever condemned to the lowest rung of the social ladder. His was an unpardonable, unforgivable crime.

Chapter Eight

True or False?

1. False. Daniel Shays supported the movement, but he had to be convinced by his friends to lead the group.

2. False. Shays was a farmer as well as a veteran of the Revolution. He was in debt, as were most farmers in western Massachusetts.

3. False. Many outspoken farmers were willing to oppose the courts. Many of them, however, had already opposed the government and had been fined or brought before the courts. Shays had a clean record, and the leaders of the movement felt that that made him a good candidate for the leadership position.

4. False. Shays did not want bloodshed. His first move was to parade with his men around the courthouse. Shays also petitioned the judges to address the farmers' grievances, but he received no satisfaction.

5. True.

6. True.

7. False. Bowdoin wanted the rebelling farmers punished. He did not listen to the debtors, nor did he advise helping to ease the debt crisis.

8. False. Shays was committed to his cause, but he did not want bloodshed. Instead, he was eager to have the General Court approve his petition or at least to open some discussion between the farmers and the legislators.

9. False. Shepard first ordered his men to fire the cannon twice over the heads of Shays's men. Shays and his men advanced closer to the arsenal after the two firings. When Shepard ordered his men to fire at the advancing farmers, Shays's men fled.

10. False. Lincoln said that he could not promise pardons for everyone. Lincoln did say he would recommend to the General Court that Shays's men be pardoned but could say nothing about Shays and his officers.

Do You Remember?

1. During the Revolution, the colonists and their leaders had closed the courts so that the judges, who were British, could not rule against the rebels. The farmers decided to use the same tactic. They believed that this would prevent further confiscation of property and imprisonment until a more equitable settlement could be reached.

2. Shays was in extreme financial straits. He had a sword already and knew that he could get good money for Lafayette's sword. He sold it to get money to feed and clothe his family.

3. The Riot Act allowed a sheriff to imprison anyone who armed himself and assembled as part of a group that did not disperse within one hour after the sheriff (reading the Riot Act) ordered it to disperse. The sheriff also had the right to confiscate the person's property and publicly whip the person.

4. Daniel Shays was respected in Pelham, Massachusetts, and was praised for the manner in which he had drilled Pelham's militia during the Revolution. Shays had attended all the conventions organized by the debtors and was widely known by those involved in the movement. Shays had supported the movement from its inception, which made him all the more trustworthy and respected by his fellow farmers.

5. Yes. On November 21, 1786, Job Shattuck, Adam Wheeler, and Henry Gale led a group of farmers to the courthouse in Worcester, Massachusetts. Job Shattuck was the only one of the three arrested and jailed in Boston. The other two escaped.

6. Putnam told Shays to give up opposing the General Court and Governor Bowdoin. He told Shays that he and his men could not win against the government officials in Boston.

7. In the Worcester Petition, Shays and his men asked the General Court to restore the right of habeas corpus, to release their comrade Job Shattuck from jail, and to pardon everyone who had armed himself to fight Massachusetts and the courts.

8. After Shays and his comrades had their first petition rejected, they submitted a second petition—the Worcester Petition (see answer 7)—which also was rejected by Governor Bowdoin. Shays realized that there was an impasse. He had no choice but to lead his men to the arsenal at Springfield and arm them in preparation for their fight to obtain justice.

9. No. The legislature chose to ignore the petitions. It probably hoped that the militia would quell the rebellion, the petitions would be forgotten, and life would continue as usual. Since the legislators owned property, their feelings probably leaned toward the creditors. Unfortunately, this made a decision on the situation even more difficult.

10. Yes. On June 13, 1788, approximately one year after the rebellion, Shays was granted a pardon.

What Do You Think?

1. During the war, the British often burned and ravaged the countryside throughout the Colonies in order to bring the colonists such hardships that they would surrender or give up the fight. In addition, many soldiers were farmers, and few farms and cultivable areas were in operation. Consequently, people turned to the large number of farmers in western Massachusetts to produce urgently needed foodstuffs and the like. The farmers, however, had to borrow money from merchants in order to increase production. When the war ended and the demand decreased, the farmers lost many of their customers and were called to repay their loans in addition to their own debts and taxes.

2. The farmers felt that they had no recourse. The courts did not listen to them even when they proved they had no money to pay their debts. The courts did not show any leniency. The farmers felt that if they objected individually, the courts would jail them individually. Many farmers were veterans of the small Continental Army that had

defeated the powerful British Army. This was their example—except the farmers preferred not to use force. They marched and had sit-ins. They petitioned and sought to resolve the matter without bloodshed.

3. The farmers did not want to be considered an extension of any other movement. They wanted the government and the courts to analyze and address their grievances. They felt that a respected, unconvicted person would get such a reaction.

4. Shays and his friends most likely felt that they did not have the time or the money to go to Boston. They were in debt and needed to farm as much as they could to pay off their debts. They also needed to do as much as possible before the courts confiscated their farms and property. Shays and his friends probably felt that their chances of success were better in surroundings they knew. They were not merchants and perhaps feared that the city might be less than hospitable to them.

5. Lafayette was a great war hero. Everyone knew how France helped win the Revolution for the patriots. To be given a sword by such a man was one of the highest honors. Selling this gift was unthinkable. His friends looked at the situation subjectively and emotionally. Shays looked at it objectively. He had a family that was hungry and debts that could deprive him of his farm, his livelihood, and his freedom (he could go to jail). Shays had to make a difficult choice, and his family, not sentiment, came first. His fellow soldiers did not have such a choice, and their judgments were ruled by their emotions.

6. Massachusetts knew that Congress had no power to enforce laws or to intervene in state matters. Massachusetts had to settle its own problems and had to quell any rebellion with its own forces. If Massachusetts allowed a person or a group to take up arms for whatever reason, anarchy would soon result. If Massachusetts allowed Shays's men to go unpunished, other groups without such justifiable reasons might follow Shays's example. The legislators felt that they had to pass a strong law to keep peace and to keep their state under control.

7. The rebels realized that they did not have the manpower or the ammunition to defeat the government's forces. They also realized that they faced prison sentences and possibly

death by hanging if their acts were judged treasonous. Shays and the farmers were law-abiding citizens. Circumstances and the terrible inequity of the debtor-creditor situation drove them to act rebelliously. They felt that they had no alternative. When they realized how unyielding the government was, they decided to lay down their arms and request a pardon rather than continue a futile struggle that could only end in bloodshed and more heartaches for their families.

8. Shepard had tried to disperse the oncoming farmers by firing over their heads. If he had allowed them to take the arsenal and the supplies within, the rebels certainly would have done so. Then the situation would have become even more critical because the farmers would have been far better armed and therefore better able to withstand or repel any militia or troops sent against them. The rebellion would have grown, and, without Congress to intervene or send troops, anarchy would have followed—maybe even secession in western Massachusetts. Shepard knew that he had to stop the rebellion at the Springfield arsenal.

9. While Shays's men were fighting for a cause in which they firmly believed, they were not soldiers fighting on a military battlefield. They had families and debts they had to pay. When they saw themselves outnumbered and at a disadvantage because of poor weapons and a lack of military supplies, they opted to withdraw rather than face certain death in an armed struggle.

10. The rebellion served its purpose by making the Massachusetts officials and its citizens aware of the inequitable debtor-creditor situation. The rebellion proved that the farmers had fought for freedom and were willing to fight to keep their freedom. Not pardoning the rebels would have made them martyrs. This would have become a rallying point for future rebels. By pardoning the rebels, the legislature was saying that it recognized the inequities and that it would try to correct the wrongs that had been committed.

From the Historical Perspective

1. Many colonists had left their European homelands because of religious, racial, or economic persecution. They also had left to escape the laws of a central power. People fought in the Revolution to protect these freedoms. Creating a central power that would govern all the states seemed hypocritical. People often chose to live in a particular state for special reasons such as religious beliefs, similar national heritage, or political philosophy. Some states condoned what others condemned. Time, however, made each state aware that the problem of power had to be resolved if the United States was to succeed. To be credible to other countries, the states had to appear as a nation that could deal with external and internal problems. This realization forced them to give Congress powers to act for the welfare of the states.

2. Before the Revolution, the American Colonies traded heavily with other colonies belonging to Britain. This was natural and quite profitable. After the Revolution, Britain hoped to hurt the states financially by cutting off these trade and economic benefits. There were quite a few people in Britain who believed that the United States would not make it on its own and would seek Britain's protection and aid. By hurting the states economically, Britain hoped to hasten the states' downfall. Imposing taxes and trade regulations would serve this purpose.

3. Shays's Rebellion clearly illustrated how powerless Congress was. Every state was having financial problems and difficulty with creditors and debtors. Since Congress had no legal right to enact laws governing all the United States, each state was forced to act independently. This led to border problems, since states enacted laws that adversely affected their neighbors. Shays's Rebellion was relatively small, but it proved that a state could rebel. This fact put the existence of the United States in jeopardy because Congress would not have had the power to quell such an uprising. Foreign powers would surely see this fault and not consider the United States a nation. Foreign powers also might hesitate to trade with the United States, causing more financial problems. A foreign nation also might decide to attack or make a treaty with one state, which would be detrimental to the nation.

Charles F. Baker is the co-founder and co-editor of *CALLIOPE* magazine and the co-author of the book *THE CLASSICAL COMPANION*. He has taught in public and private schools and is an administrator in the New Bedford Public School System in Massachusetts.

Cobblestone Publishing publishes three history-related magazines for the 8- to 15-year-old reader.

COBBLESTONE offers a thematic approach to American history.

FACES, published in cooperation with the American Museum of Natural History, encourages a deeper appreciation for other cultures.

CALLIOPE covers world history, from ancient times to the Renaissance.

All three magazines are unique in basing each issue on a single theme and in maintaining a continuous list of back issues. For more information, including a complete list of more than 200 back issues, write to Cobblestone Publishing, 30 Grove St., Peterborough, NH 03458.